D1474301

# Go for Wand

# Go for Wand

*by* BILL HELLER

Lexington, Kentucky

Library of Congress Card Number: 00-101133

ISBN 1-58150-046-7

Printed in The United States
First Edition: July 2000

a division of
The Blood-Horse, Inc.
PUBLISHERS SINCE 1916

To learn more about Go for Wand and other classic Thoroughbreds, see:

www.thoroughbredlegends.com

# Go for Wand

# Contents

# Go for Wand

## INTRODUCTION

### *A Saratoga Reflection*

She should have stopped. When she hit the top of the stretch in the 1990 Test Stakes at Saratoga, Go for Wand should have packed it in. She hadn't raced in fifty-three days, one of the reasons being a cough which caused her to miss a week and a half of training. She was hooking the best three-year-old filly sprinters in the country and had broken eighth in a field of ten in a grade I stakes. She had dragged jockey Randy Romero to battle Forest Fealty on the lead through a :22 1/5 opening quarter and a suicidal half in :44 3/5. She had taken a narrow lead over Forest Fealty only to lose it back to her. The rest of the field was closing in for the kill.

But Go for Wand just kept going. She spurted away and won the Test by two lengths in 1:21, tying Very Subtle's stakes record and missing Darby Creek Road's track record for seven furlongs by three-fifths of a second.

Her trainer, Billy Badgett, was stunned by her performance. She was even better winning the grade I Alabama Stakes nine days later, drawing off to a seven-length victory and running the fastest Alabama in its 110-year history despite being wrapped up by Romero twenty yards from the wire. Badgett smiled at the memory. "Effortless," he said. "Randy never even asked her to run."

Romero would. Later that year, he would.

Separating triumph and tragedy is an arduous endeavor, but remembering only Go for Wand's shocking, public death in the 1990 Breeders' Cup Distaff robs her of all the accomplishments of her life. After the Alabama, she humbled older fillies and mares in both the Maskette and Beldame, her fifth and sixth grade I stakes victories in a phenomenal three-year-old season which earned her a second consecutive Eclipse Award. She took a career record of ten wins and two seconds in twelve starts into her fateful showdown with another distaff champion, Bayakoa, in a match-up that could have decided Horse of the Year. Instead, it ended Go for Wand's life, when she broke down in deep stretch trying to cling to a slight lead she had worked so hard to earn, snapping her right ankle in front of more than 50,000 fans and a national television audience of millions.

"It wasn't her tragic death that meant so much, it was her joy of racing," her owner, Jane du Pont Lunger, the matriarch of Christiana Stables, said. "She was doing what she wanted to do. She could have broken down in the stall, for that matter. I don't like people to remember the tragedy of her death."

It is a warm August afternoon in 1999 and Mrs. Lunger, who has lived in Wilmington, Delaware, for most her life, is at her favorite place in the world: her box seats at Saratoga Race Course, where she has attended the annual summer meet for three-quarters of her eighty-five years. "Sixty-three years at Saratoga," she said. "I missed two years when I had a baby."

Maybe 200 yards away, her great filly is buried in the infield. To get there, one would have to walk into the winner's circle and cross the most famous dirt track in the world, the one where Man o' War and Secretariat were defeated. It is the same track where Go for Wand, the daughter of an amazing twenty-two-year-old broodmare, displayed her brilliance in the Test and Alabama.

She was a once in a lifetime filly and she knew it.

"She was always extremely intelligent," Rose Badgett, Badgett's wife and Go for Wand's exercise rider and confidante, said. "You could sit on her and she'd notice a plane going by. She'd look up. Most horses don't even notice that stuff. When I worked her, at the eighth pole, I used to stand there all day."

Rose Badgett demonstrated her affection for the filly, petting her and indulging Go for Wand's fondness for standing and looking. On race days, an outrider would lead the filly to the backside so she could stand quietly for a few minutes. Said Badgett: "She never got rattled. She'd take a deep breath and just stand there, kind of like a good athlete when they're getting ready."

Then she would grunt. "Two or three minutes before the race, she would grunt like a hog," Romero said. "She did it almost every time. I've never heard anything like that in my life. I firmly believe she was getting herself psyched."

Off the track, "Wanda" had other priorities. "As soon as she would hear Rose's voice, she would start nickering," Badgett said. "It was pretty amazing. But then, Rose would always have a bag of carrots."

That was only one of Wanda's habits. "We used to take her out to graze at three o'clock every afternoon,"

Badgett said. "Every day at three o'clock, she'd come to the front of the stall and start hollering at you that it was time for her to go. You could set your watch to it. She was pretty exceptional. She knew that she was special, which was probably the nicest part of being around her. To me, to be able to train a horse like that, is just something I'll never forget as long as I live."

Go for Wand's bittersweet story was woven in the tapestry of human drama surrounding her. Billy Badgett, her soft-spoken and vastly underrated trainer, was, and still is, no stranger to unexpected sadness on the backstretch. He and Rose were engaged just before Go for Wand won the 1989 Breeders' Cup Juvenile Fillies and married twenty-one days before the 1990 Breeders' Cup, delaying their honeymoon until after the race. Few people knew that Rose was carrying the Badgetts' first child as she continued to exercise Go for Wand every morning right up to that race.

Randy Romero, the only jockey she ever had, was, perhaps, the toughest rider ever to walk out of a jockey's room. No jockey endured more pain maintaining a career. He suffered broken ribs when Go for Wand went down, then came back to the track and rode later that day in another

Breeders' Cup race. His career, however, was never the same. But his career never would have included Go for Wand had he not had the good fortune of being at the Badgett barn one morning at Saratoga when Badgett needed someone to exercise her. He asked Romero. And Badgett, who mostly used Jerry Bailey or Mike Smith as his rider then, never took Romero off Go for Wand.

Mrs. Lunger, whose husband helped pioneer racing in the state of Delaware, never let her allergy to horses, her husband's death, or the loss of Go for Wand prevent her from bringing a still vibrant Christiana Stables into a new century.

The Badgetts have continued their success in New York, too, never losing their passion for racing. Rose still exercises horses for her husband six days a week and tends to their three children. It is a hard life she and Billy still embrace. "There are people out there who work nine to five in office buildings," she said. "We're out there on the ponies, talking to friends, enjoying being outside. There are some days you wouldn't change anything."

*Bill Heller*

*Albany, New York, 2000*

# CHAPTER I

## A Foundation In Delaware

Go for Wand's brilliant career was the culmination of more than fifty years that Harry W. and Jane du Pont Lunger devoted to horses. Harry Lunger, an attorney and stockbroker, was a graduate of Princeton University and the Harvard Law School who did legal work for the Delaware State Legislature. He was instrumental in bringing pari-mutuel racing to Delaware and in the opening of Delaware Park in 1937. "At that time, for someone to say we're going to have legal racing was like you saying, 'Well, come on, let's go to Mars for lunch,' " Mrs. Lunger said.

Her ancestors didn't come quite that far. She is the sixth generation of Pierre Samuel du Pont de Nemours, who emigrated from France to the United States, arriving on New Year's Day, 1800. His son founded the famed du Pont chemical company. Mrs. Lunger's great-grandfather, Alexis, was the last family member connected with the company.

The Lungers raised five children, Philip, Brett, Ann, David, and Mary, on their 100-acre property, a former dairy farm, outside Wilmington.

"Harry said, 'When we have racing in Delaware, I'll buy a horse,' " Mrs. Lunger related sixty-two years later. "And I said, 'Oh yes.' And he did. He was always terribly enthusiastic about racing. And he had almost a sixth sense when it came to bloodlines."

*Daily Racing Form* columnist Joe Hirsch once described Harry Lunger as "a wonderful man with a keen grasp of pedigree." But the Lunger's first horse, Brook, was awful. "He never beat a horse," Mrs. Lunger said. "He ran and ran forever, but he never beat a horse. Then, from there, we started."

Well after Christiana had established itself as a successful stable, none other than Pulitzer Prize winner Red Smith devoted his syndicated column of September 18, 1961 to the Lungers, conjuring headlines such as:

*Although Brook Never Beat A Horse*

*The Lungers Decided To Branch Out*

After noting Brook's lack of success, Smith wrote, "Instead of giving up, the Lungers branched out. They sought out the advice of the late Jack Healey, a great horseman. Pretty soon, relying on his judgment, they had horses fast enough to finish next-to-last. At last the day came when Harry and Jane Lunger, swelling with happiness and pride, watched a boy wearing the yellow and purple silks cantering back to the winner's circle."

There have been a lifetime of winners for Mrs. Lunger despite her paradoxical allergy to horses. "She gets allergies; she has never been an equestrian person," said her son-in-law, Richard Jones, a lawyer who has managed Christiana Stables with Mrs. Lunger since Harry Lunger passed away at the age of seventy-one on July 31, 1976. "They always said if Delaware Park hadn't opened, they would have bought a second sailboat. It was kind of a lark."

Mrs. Lunger explained her allergy: "My husband loved to go on riding trips out West, and he used to insist that I go, too. I hated it. As soon as we started out, I'd get a headache. I didn't even like to go to the racetrack, because I felt so awful there. Then, after years went by, it was discovered that I was allergic. I

have to be very careful, even going to visit the horses in the stable, which I like to do. When I go into the winner's circle, I push the horse aside."

The Lungers chose to race in a stable name, and their choice of Christiana reflects the Swedish influence in the colonization of Delaware in the 1600s. When Delaware was originally settled, the land was divided into parcels. Each was restricted to 100 families. The Christiana Hundred was named after Queen Christiana of Sweden.

Undeterred by Brook's lack of success on the racetrack, the Lungers purchased a yearling filly named Miss Ferdinand for $7,000, a considerable amount of money in 1938. "She was by Bull Dog," Mrs. Lunger said. "And that was the beginning. We raced eight or nine generations of her offspring. Harry almost had a sixth sense when he bought a horse. He was wild about Miss Ferdinand's bloodlines, but he also was an awfully good judge of a horse. He liked her conformation."

Miss Ferdinand didn't take long to compensate for Brook's failures. The daughter of Sweep out of Misleading won the $17,400 Matron Stakes at Belmont Park and the Saratoga Speed Stakes in 1939. She also enabled Mrs. Lunger to get a portrait of Harry Lunger.

"Harry had a portrait made of me and one of the children, and I told him it was time to get his made," Mrs. Lunger told Tracy Gantz in a 1979 story in *The Blood-Horse*. "He said, 'no,' but that he would when we won our first stakes. So when Miss Ferdinand won the Matron, she was leading down the old Widener Chute about two-thirds of the way up. I turned to Harry and said, 'Listen, you get me that portrait right now.' He said, 'I thought you'd remember that.' I got the portrait, too — it was rotten."

In 1943, Miss Ferdinand produced Sea Snack, the Lunger's first homebred stakes winner, who won thirteen of thirty-eight starts and earned $127,400. Sea Snack, in turn, produced Endine, who won successive runnings of the Delaware Handicap in 1958 and '59 and made $306,547, and stakes winners Ricci Tavi and Water Twister.

Mrs. Lunger found great delight in naming her horses and she did not mind asking for assistance. "I try desperately to get good names," she said. "I think we have good names, and we have help. Every year we give out a little booklet to our friends, and it gives the breeding of everything we have. Anybody who can submit a name that will be accepted gets a free $10 win bet the first time the horse runs. We had a Thinking Cap—Love Time filly, and a man at The Jockey Club said, 'Well, why don't you call her Park Now (for Love Time). So we named her Park Now and she won her first race at about 10-1. I sent the guy a check for $115. He had forgotten about it, and he was just ecstatic."

Mrs. Lunger said that Sea Snack was one of her best names. "Sea Snack was out of Miss Ferdinand by Hard Tack, which was from Tea Biscuit," she said. "In the service, when you had hard tack, you ate it. And if you were a sailor, you could consider it a sea snack."

Endine was named for a sea nymph, but Mrs. Lunger confessed that she spelled the name wrong. It should have been Ondine.

"Then we had a full sister to Sea Snack named Bride's Biscuit," Mrs. Lunger said. "Bride's Biscuit had a mare called Home to Mama because the bride's biscuit was so hard that the husband went home to mama."

The Lungers also purchased Miss Ferdinand's half-sister, Camargo. Camargo produced Thinking Cap, a small horse barely fifteen hands tall who won the 1955 Travers Stakes and Lawrence Realization. Unfortunately, the Lungers missed that Travers, which she calls their most prestigious victory. "We were on a ship coming back from Europe and were told about it," she said. Miss Ferdinand and Camargo became Christiana's foundation broodmares.

One of the stakes races Thinking Cap lost was the 1956 Exterminator Handicap — to another Christiana horse, Ricci Tavi. "Ricci Tavi and Thinking Cap ran together in a race that our trainer, Henry Clark, wanted to win very badly in Maryland," Mrs. Lunger said. "Ricci Tavi won the race, and I burst into tears because the wrong horse won. I didn't like Ricci as well as Thinking Cap. I was absolutely heartbroken. I went down to the winner's circle, they gave me the trophy, and the tears were streaming down my face. The proof of the pudding is that the Cyane—Thinking Cap combination has produced an awful lot of stakes winners."

Mrs. Lunger was particularly proud of Christiana horses that won stakes in her backyard, Delaware Park. "I love racing at Delaware Park," she said. "It's a nice country track, well run, and it's very convenient. I can be there in fourteen minutes if I put my mind to it. My two favorite tracks are Delaware Park and Saratoga."

Most of the time. "We won the Delaware Handicap and the Delaware Oaks four times each, but we were disqualified once in the Oaks (in 1969)," Mrs. Lunger said in a 1979 interview. "Harry went down to receive the trophy. Nobody thought we would lose it, because both jockeys were all over the track. The filly was Pit Bunny, which was named that because one of my sons is a race-car driver. She was known as a 'house horse' because Harry was a director at the track. There was a long delay, and I know they took it away from us mainly because it was a house horse."

Though she'd beaten Gallant Bloom by a length and a quarter, Pit Bunny had been disqualified and placed second. Gallant Bloom went on to be named champion three-year-old filly.

"We went back to the stable, and Harry was sitting in the car looking at the horse," Mrs. Lunger said. "He said to Henry (trainer Henry Clark), 'Well, we beat her anyway. They took it away from us, but we did beat her."

Mrs. Lunger said Christiana's most popular horse in Delaware was Light Hearted, who won six consecutive races at Delaware Park, including the Oaks. "She was a heroine among the Delaware people, and that was exciting," Mrs. Lunger said. "I love to win in my own state because it makes me feel good for the public and for my friends. Christiana has a good name, and it's important that we maintain a high standard in racing."

Miss Ferdinand and Camargo allowed Christiana to do that, becoming Christiana's foundation broodmares. Of the Lungers' first twenty-six added-money winners, seventeen of them traced their pedigree to either Miss Ferdinand or Camargo.

They reflect the importance of broodmares in Christiana's substantial success. Mrs. Lunger sells most of her colts and tries to keep a good percentage of her fillies to become future broodmares. "I have to sell the colts so that I can afford to keep the fillies," she said. "Racing is a business. It has to be. But it is also a sport, and I think the two can be combined very gracefully. You can be a lady and sportsman, but still know when to buy and sell."

Accordingly, she set her standards high for determining which Christiana fillies would be retained to become broodmares. One of the most important crite-

rion is heart. A filly doesn't necessarily have to win, but she has to try in order to earn a place in the Christiana broodmare band. "A lot of people ask me why I'm willing to breed a horse that has not been raced," she noted. "If she's shown speed, I don't mind at all. If you breed a filly that you know has absolutely no heart, that is chicken, I think you're wasting your time. I'd rather have a horse that will really try and maybe not win the big ones, but be in contention."

For an example in a 1979 interview, she offered Croquis, a daughter of Arts and Letters whose fourth dam back was none other than Sea Snack. Mrs. Lunger shipped Croquis down from Saratoga in 1979 to race in the Delaware Oaks. "She hadn't been on the track one day, and she just couldn't get the feel of the track," Mrs. Lunger said. "But she tried every inch of the way. If she never raced again she would be fine in my book for breeding because she showed me she had tenacity, heart, courage."

And she did pass that trait on to her progeny, producing Gold Alert, a stakes-winning son of Mr. Prospector, one of the more than forty stakes winners Christiana has raced in a span stretching nearly sixty years. Thirty of them were homebreds. Christiana also bred Tempted, the 1959 champion handicap mare, who raced for Mrs. Lunger's mother, Mrs. Philip du Pont. Tempted won eighteen of forty-five races, including the Jeanne d'Arc Stakes at two in 1957, and the Maskette, Alabama, and Jersey Belle Stakes at three, when she also equaled the track record at Delaware Park for one mile (1:37 1/5). At four, she won nine of thirteen starts, including the Ladies Handicap, when she set an American record of 2:02 3/5 for one and five-sixteenths miles while carrying 128 pounds. Tempted earned $330,760 and produced the stakes winner Lead Me On.

Gold Alert won the Eclipse and Dominion Day Handicap as a four-year-old in 1987, and his maternal line is all Christiana homebreds: Croquis out of Unity Hall (a daughter of Cyane) out of Rum Bottle Bay (a daughter of Thinking Cap) out of Sea Snack out of Miss Ferdinand. Rum Bottle Bay produced six winners, including three stakes winners, from seven foals. Unity Hall produced six winners, three of them stakes winners, from eight foals. Gold Alert was the third winner from Croquis' first seven foals and her first stakes winner.

Christiana's success was built on generations of suc-

cessful broodmares. But Mrs. Lunger defers the credit to her husband: "Harry felt so strongly about the bloodlines. He was the one who decided all of the matings, and he was highly successful at it. My enjoyment with the stable is more the enthusiasm of the people. I love the month at Saratoga. I love the yearling sales. I love the connections with the horses — knowing the breeders, the owners, and the jockeys."

And, of course, the trainers.

The Lungers' first trainer was Selby Burch, Hall of Fame trainer Preston Burch's brother. Selby Burch, who died in 1941, was followed by John A. "Jack" Healey, Christiana's main trainer until his death in 1947. The Lungers then began a long, rewarding relationship with Hall of Famer Henry Clark. Billy Badgett wouldn't be born for another five years.

"I had a lot of trainers in my day," Mrs. Lunger said. "Of course, my favorite was Henry Clark. He was just so super, a real friend as well as a good trainer. All my trainers have been real friends."

The feeling was mutual. Clark enjoyed the family spirit the Lungers literally brought to the racetrack, when pictures in the winner's circle of a Christiana horse were taken with a horde of Lunger grandchildren. "I have a winner's circle picture at home in which Jane was no bigger than her grandchildren," Clark said in a 1981 story in *Daily Racing Form*. "It's wonderful to see the kids grow up and take an interest in breeding and racing. Mr. Lunger was a real student of bloodlines. The success that Christiana has had over the years is attributable to his judgment."

Clark, who passed away in 1999 at the age of ninety-five, trained many outstanding horses for Christiana, including Thinking Cap and Linkage, who won the Blue Grass Stakes twenty-seven years after Thinking Cap's Travers.

Go for Wand's pedigree traces back to another Clark-trained, Christiana star, Cyane. In 1960, the Lungers purchased the son of Turn-to out of Your Game by Beau Pere at the Saratoga yearling sale for $34,000. Cyane was the name of the ship Mrs. Lunger's grandfather commanded during the Civil War. Cyane won the 1961 Futurity and 1962 Dwyer Handicap, earning $176,367 before being retired to stud. He stood at various farms in Maryland and Virginia and sired Smarten, Maryland's leading sire in 1989.

Cyane's first yearling offered at public sale was a filly out of the mare Book of Verse, a daughter of One Count. The Cyane filly appeared in the 1966 Saratoga yearling sale and the Lungers purchased her for $15,000, which surprised their trainer, Clark, who had not yet seen the filly. "Henry was upset because he hadn't had a chance to look at her first," Mrs. Lunger said. "But Mr. Lunger was determined. He said we had to support our stallion." According to Jones, more than two decades later, Mrs. Lunger would pay a commission to the retired Clark, as if he were the trainer, every time the Cyane filly's daughter, Go for Wand, won.

Mrs. Lunger named the Cyane filly. Eventually.

"She'll send two-year-olds to be trained, but won't name them," Jones said. "She said, 'As long as I don't name them, they can't run them.'"

She once explained her thinking: "I seldom name a horse before he's two. That just drives everybody crazy, but I want to get something I really think is appropriate. I want a real reason. I want to know a horse's personality before I name it. This is very hard on The Jockey Club and they're after me to name them sooner."

She took her time with the Cyane filly. The Lungers

once built a home in Jamaica, and Mrs. Lunger, who is deeply superstitious, had heard of a West Indies myth where natives fear the Obeah Man and the Obeah Woman because they have the power to cast spells. Mrs. Lunger named the Cyane filly Obeah. Mrs. Lunger's superstitions include liking the number "thirteen," never putting a hat on a bed, and making certain that certain people sit in certain places when certain horses race.

Obeah earned $387,299 and won three major stakes at Delaware Park: the Delaware Handicap twice and the Blue Hen Stakes, as well as the Vineland Handicap at Garden State and the Firenze Handicap at Aqueduct. She finished second in the Beldame Stakes, the Firenze, the Diana Handicap at Saratoga, the Stymie Handicap at Belmont taking on colts, and the Jeanne d'Arc Stakes at Narragansett. She was third in the Frizette Stakes, Firenze, and Ladies Handicap at Aqueduct and finished her four-year racing career with eleven wins in forty-six starts.

Obeah did even better as a broodmare after she retired in late 1970. Being bred to Northern Dancer didn't hurt. "When she first retired, Northern Dancer was just getting going," Jones said. "He stood at

Windfields Farm in Maryland. We bred her five times to him, the first time for $20,000 or $25,000. The fifth time it went up to $50,000. We subsequently paid $100,000 to breed a different mare to him. After that, the fee went out of sight."

By then, Obeah was on her way to an incredible run as a broodmare, producing ten winners from her first eleven foals. Her first two foals, both by Northern Dancer, were black-type winners. Black Powder, her first foal born in 1972, raced for eight years, winning twenty-seven of his 118 starts, including the $17,842 E. Palmer Heagerty Stakes at Bowie. He was also third in the Allegheny Stakes.

Obeah's second foal, a 1973 colt named Dance Spell, was even better. He won seven of twenty-five starts and $326,090. A fierce competitor who excelled at one mile, Dance Spell won two grade II stakes at that distance, the Jerome Handicap and Saranac Stakes, in addition to the ungraded Jamaica Handicap. He was second in the Woodward, Champagne, Remsen, Jim Dandy, and Rockaway Stakes, and third in the Travers, Laurel Futurity, and Dwyer Handicap. He sired sixty-six foals before breaking his back in a paddock accident.

Dance Spell's progeny included Broom Dance out of Witching Hour by Thinking Cap. Witching Hour was bred by the Lungers and won three races before producing two additional homebred stakes winners, Salem and Tingle Stone, named for one of the magic stones of Stonehenge in England, as well as Pumpkin Moonshine, whom the Lungers sold and did not race. Incredibly, Salem, Tingle Stone, and Pumpkin Moonshine's career earnings were nearly identical. Salem won $203,488; Tingle Stone won $196,571 and Pumpkin Moonshine $199,910.

Broom Dance, whose five stakes victories included the grade I Alabama in 1982, is the dam of End Sweep, a multiple stakes winner in 1994 who was the leading first-crop sire in 1998 and now stands in Japan. In April of 2000 he was atop the third-crop sire list by progeny earnings, thanks to Flamingo Stakes winner Trippi.

Obeah was matched with Graustark and Hoist the Flag, producing two colts in the span of three years (1974-1976) — she was barren one year — who did little on the racetrack: Bleaky, a winner in Mexico, and Magic Banner, a non-winner. Christiana decided to go back to Northern Dancer, and Obeah produced two more winners: a 1977 colt named Voodoo Rhythm,

who won four of eleven starts and $64,900 before beginning a stud career in Australia, and in 1978, her first filly, Discorama, who was a major stakes winner. Discorama captured the grade II Gazelle Handicap and the Wistful Stakes; was second in the grade I Ladies Handicap, and finished third in the grade I Top Flight Handicap and Alabama Stakes and in the then-grade II Test Stakes. She won five of seventeen starts in her two-year racing career and earned $181,569.

But Discorama was the last top foal Obeah produced for several years. East Is East, a 1979 colt by Damascus, won one race and became a stallion in Argentina. Obeah was not bred the following year and then was sent for the final time to Northern Dancer. The 1981 colt from that mating, Carnivalay, won one of just four starts. After being barren again, Obeah was matched twice with Assert, producing a 1984 filly, Throw Away Line, who won one race in seventeen starts, and a 1985 filly named Assertaine, who won one race in four starts. The following season, Obeah was barren.

Two of the times Obeah was barren, she had been covered by Nijinsky II, a son of Northern Dancer, according to Jones. Consequently, Jones said he thought a change was needed. "I had developed a rule of thumb," he said. "If we have a mare anywhere who doesn't get in foal two years, we move her to another farm."

The Lungers once tried keeping horses on their Delaware estate, but it did not go well. "We didn't have the facilities to do it right," Mrs. Lunger said. "Alexis (named after Alexis du Pont), the only horse we ever ran in the Kentucky Derby, was one of the few horses we ever kept here. Some deer hunters were shooting and a bullet ricocheted and went through one of his legs. We decided this wasn't the right place for our horses."

Obeah wound up in Pennsylvania, although she was sent to Maryland to be bred to Deputy Minister, a grandson of Northern Dancer. Jones was not terribly optimistic. "Obeah was quite old when she foaled Go for Wand," he said. "In the back of your mind, you're saying that's against her. Sometimes, older mares don't pass on certain nutritional things."

Go for Wand was foaled on April 6, 1987, at Walnut Green Farm in Unionville, Pennsylvania, co-owned by Richard Jones and his brother, Russell Jones Jr. She didn't stay there for long, going to Claiborne Farm in Kentucky, where she eventually was broken. Go for

Wand then went to Camden, South Carolina, where she came under the care of Jamie Woodington who had most of Badgett's yearlings.

A friend of Mrs. Lunger's suggested a name. As the legend of the Obeah Man and the Obeah Woman is told in Jamaica, when one of them appears, natives must run back to their homes and find a wand to ward off the spirits. Mrs. Lunger settled on Go for Wand.

Go for Wand was a rugged, striking foal with a long, narrow white blaze down her face. Those who remember her described her as having great presence and a certain majesty.

Said Jones: "There was something so special about her."

# Go for Wand

# CHAPTER 2

## Billy

Billy Badgett Jr. is unusually quiet and reluctant to draw attention to himself. He has carved a niche training in New York with little fanfare, though he campaigned Go for Wand masterfully and has consistently turned out stakes winners before and after her, frequently getting the most out of modestly priced yearlings. "I call him 'Bang for the Buck Badgett' because he's taking $65,000 and $75,000 horses and beating the pants off some of these million-dollar babies," one of his owners, Peter Callahan, said in Jay Hovdey's column in the *Daily Racing Form*, September 24, 1999.

Callahan, a publishing executive, has firsthand knowledge. Badgett and Callahan bought Bevo for $75,000 and he capped his two-year-old season by winning the 1999 grade I Futurity at Belmont Park over previously undefeated More Than Ready, subsequent grade I stakes winner Greenwood Lake, and Chief Seattle, who subsequently ran second to Anees in the Breeders' Cup Juvenile. But Badgett had little time to celebrate the victory by Bevo, whose second dam, Family Way, was bred by Christiana Stables.

Badgett watched the replay in the clubhouse, celebrated with a beer, and headed for the backstretch, where he noticed Bevo taking a couple of awkward steps walking on the road outside the barn. "I said it was definitely his foot, but when he got in the stall, all of a sudden the blood started going to the area where he got hurt," Badgett said. "So we X rayed it right away."

The X rays revealed Bevo had a bone chip in his left knee. He was done for the year.

"We've all gone through it, and, obviously, things are going to happen, but the toughest part is that it's like Charismatic two jumps after the wire in the Belmont. And Grindstone. And Flanders. The list goes on and on," Badgett said. "Unfortunately, the good horses who try a hundred times harder than your average, every-day horse — and that's why they're good horses — seem to get hurt a little more severely because they're running on guts and determination and heart and desire. So when something goes on them, it usually goes a little bit worse than if a horse just pulled up. They kind of run right through the pain, like good running backs or good basketball players. They hurt the knee, but they keep playing."

All of twenty-five days later, Badgett was preparing Nitecap, another two-year-old owned by Callahan, for a possible start in the Cowdin Stakes. The $160,000 purchase had only two starts, winning a maiden race impressively. Nitecap was working five-eighths of a mile on the main track at Belmont with Rose in the saddle when he fractured both sesamoid bones in his right foreleg. He died.

Rose wasn't injured, and the Badgetts re-grouped and continued. That's what horsemen do. They continue. It goes with the territory, and Badgett has lived in that territory his whole life. In spite of the hard times, it is a life he still enjoys: "Especially when you always look forward to, hopefully, coming up with a good horse year after year. You never know where they're going to come from, like Bevo.

We bought him at a yearling sale, for not a lot of money. It was kind of fun watching him grow and develop as a young horse. That's the fun part of the game for me."

Since he was a child, Badgett has enjoyed the game. Born July 3, 1952, in Mineola, Long Island, Badgett was one of five children, the only one who followed his father into horse racing and stayed. One of his brothers, Tracy, was a jockey's agent for two years, but is now out of the business and working in construction.

Badgett's dad, William, is known as Zeke and was raised in Kentucky. Zeke Badgett began riding when he was about thirteen and rode until he was seventeen. "He rode in New Orleans, Detroit, Kentucky, around that circuit," Badgett said. "Then he just got too big."

Zeke went to work for Hall of Fame trainer Woody Stephens — Billy Badgett would, too — and was with him for eighteen years. For nine of those years, Stephens was the private trainer for Harry Guggenheim and his powerful Cain Hoy Stable. "I grew up on the Guggenheim Estate out in Port Washington (Long Island), where my dad broke the yearlings for Woody,"

Badgett said. In the winter, Badgett's dad accompanied the yearlings to their winter home in Columbia, South Carolina. "I kind of grew up on the racetrack, a racetrack brat more or less," Badgett said. "I really enjoyed the horses."

He figures he was six or seven when he got on a horse for the first time. "Then when I was twelve or thirteen, I started getting on the yearlings when they were being broken," he said. "Before school in the mornings, I'd get on a couple. They were turned out during the day, and when I came home from school, we used to bring them in. It was a great experience."

Badgett went to Springfield College in Massachusetts for a year, but his heart was with the horses. His decision to leave school initially disappointed his father, but Zeke Badgett ultimately gave his blessings.

Now, Badgett is supportive of his father, who helps him out around the barn.

At age nineteen, Badgett began working for Dominic Imperio, his first of three lengthy engagements as he honed his craft. He started at the bottom of the ladder, as a hotwalker. "I worked for Dominic for about five years and then I worked for Joe Cantey for

five years," Badgett said. "Joe was a very, very good horseman. With Joe, everything was military like. Everything was 5:30, 6 o'clock, 6:30, 7. Everything was in order. He was very strict, time-wise. Everything was in place. Everything ran to the letter. Woody was a little more laid back. Woody was a very competitive person, which people didn't realize about him at all. He was extremely competitive. And Joe was a hundred times more competitive than Woody. Joe was a little bit harder, but he was a very, very good trainer."

Badgett's career path crossed Stephens' after the trainer's brother, Bill, who had broken all of Stephens' yearlings in South Carolina for years, became ill. "We were at the gap one day on the track," Badgett said. "And Woody asked me what I was doing, if I was happy with Joe. I was kind of ready to make a move. I'd been there for a long time and things weren't really changing as far as me going out on my own. So I figured it was worth a shot. So I went to work for Woody. He was a tremendous person to work for. Five years there was worth its weight in gold."

Badgett broke all of Stephens' yearlings for five years in Aiken, South Carolina, much like his father had before him. Badgett couldn't have picked a better time. It was the early 1980s, and Stephens' barn was full of stars: Swale, Devil's Bag, Miss Oceana, Stephan's Odyssey, Creme Fraiche, and Caveat. "We were on a serious roll when I was there," Badgett said. "I was lucky to be there when all his horses were hitting. I was lucky to have them in Aiken, too, before they came up."

Nothing topped winning five consecutive Belmont Stakes, a phenomenal training accomplishment which forever will link Woody Stephens' name to greatness. Badgett missed the first one with Conquistador Cielo in 1982, but was there for Caveat, Swale, Creme Fraiche, and Danzig Connection, who won the 1986 edition.

Badgett had an insightful anecdote about Danzig Connection. "Jerry Bailey was riding him in an allowance race about nine days before the Peter Pan," Badgett said. "I didn't think he could lose, but a horse of Oscar Barrera's beat him. Bailey hit him like twenty-five times down the stretch. Boom, boom. Left handed. Just relentless. I was very upset that he got beat. And Woody says:

'Did you see anything today?'

'Not really, boss.'

'He come back all right?'

'Yeah, he's fine. Actually, he's probably a little upset he got beat.'

'You know why he got beat?'

'No.'

'He didn't want to get hit with that whip.' "

Badgett raced to the steward's stand and asked if he could watch the replay. He watched the re-run five times. "The horse, every time Bailey hit him, pinned his ears back and kept pulling himself up," Badgett said. "He kept swinging his tail when he's hit. Woody picked up on it. I didn't. He was phenomenal about stuff like that. He just picked up on things. He calls in Pat Day for the Peter Pan and says, 'I don't care what happens, I don't want you to hit this horse. Don't hit him. Even if you get tempted, drop the stick. I don't care what you do. Don't hit him.' He never hit him. He galloped. Same thing for the Belmont (when Chris McCarron rode him). Never hit him. He didn't want to be touched with the whip. It was amazing."

Some Belmont Stakes memories are better than others. Swale and Devil's Bag were born the same year, and both wound up in Stephens' barn. Devil's Bag was sensational as a two-year-old, while Swale was very good, but less flashy. "I had a bet with Phil Gleaves (also one of Stephens' assistants)," Badgett said. "I said, 'This horse is a better horse than Devil's Bag. Believe me what I tell you.' " Badgett had a reason for that feeling. "I was working on Devil's Bag's shins every day relentlessly," he said. "He just had chronic shins. He was a good horse, a phenomenal two-year-old. But Swale was always there, winning by a head, winning by a neck, winning the Young America at the Meadowlands by a zop (nose). As they made the transition from two to three, you could see Swale moving ahead of that other horse by leaps and bounds. And, unfortunately, that other horse didn't stay sound. But I mean Swale just galloped in the Derby."

But not in the Preakness. "Woody had been sick and Swale breezed a half-mile in like :46 three days before the Preakness," Badgett said. Swale finished seventh in the Preakness.

Badgett dismissed that effort, noticing that Swale was fatigued when he got back to Belmont Park. "But

about seven or eight days after the Preakness, he started coming around. He was really doing very, very well for the Belmont," Badgett recalled.

Swale did win the Belmont wire to wire under Laffit Pincay Jr.

Eight days later, Badgett walked Swale back to the barn after a morning gallop. "The horse was doing tremendous," Badgett said.

The colt was cooled out and led from the barn for his bath. Badgett was sitting nearby on a fence, watching him.

In an instant, Swale jumped into the air and literally dropped dead. "Believe me, he was dead when he hit the ground," Badgett said. "He had to have some kind of seizure or some kind of blockage. They did an autopsy on him and never found anything wrong. I've seen horses get hurt and break down, but I was just in shock. You never expect that to happen."

Stephens had been set to take the first vacation of his life with his loving wife, Lucille. They had decided to celebrate the Belmont Stakes victory with a trip to Alaska. Badgett had the painful task of calling Stephens and telling him what happened: "He was devastated, obviously, but he got on the phone and called Seth

(Hancock of Claiborne Farm, which owned Swale). Stephens said, 'You're not going to believe what just happened.' Seth told him, 'Woody, just go get on the plane and go on your vacation. There's nothing you can do about it now.' "

Stephens handled the loss and went about winning two more Belmont Stakes, with Creme Fraiche and Danzig Connection. Through his five-year tenure with the Hall of Fame trainer, Badgett culled many bits of wisdom, not only about dealing with horses, but about dealing with people, too. "Believe me, in five years, the guy never raised his voice. Never," Badgett said. "If he got upset with you, he'd call you in his office. Sit you down. Never say anything to you in the barn in front of anybody else. Never got mad. And that kind of went over to his horses, too. Always kill them with kindness, kill them with kindness. He never got upset with his horses. If something happened, if he had a bad actor, he always worked around it."

That was one of many lessons Badgett learned from Stephens. "I learned lessons from him about developing young horses because he was a master

at that," Badgett said. "And that each horse is an individual and that you treat him like that. You try to do what's best for your horses. Spot him in the right places. The list goes on and on. And then, once you go on your own, everything completely changes anyway. But it always helps. You always go back to the basics."

After five years, Badgett felt that it was time to become his own boss. His current boss was reluctant to see him go. "He wanted me to stay there until he retired," Badgett recalled. "I said, 'Boss, that's going to be like waiting for you to die. I don't want that to happen. I don't want to see you die, and obviously I don't want to wait until you retire another ten years from now before I take over what's probably not going to be a lot left anyway.' Which is exactly what happened. So he kind of understood all that."

Stephens, however, didn't understand why Badgett left to train for Peter Blum. "He says, 'You're making a big mistake going to work for him. He's not the kind of person that you want to start off with,'" Badgett said. "And sure enough, eight months later, the guy fired me. Woody said, 'I told you son, I told you.' "

But Stephens wasn't done helping Badgett. Stephens not only gave him a couple of his own second string horses, but convinced a couple of his clients to do the same, allowing Badgett to build a small stable of eight horses.

Then Badgett got better ones through contacts he had made working for Stephens, notably Seth Hancock. "Seth was very instrumental in me getting Christiana," Badgett said. "And he was very instrumental in me getting Greentree, two of the biggest outfits in the country. And that was from the exposure of working for Stephens."

It's an experience Badgett will never forget. "It's nice when you go to work every day, and you enjoy going to work," Badgett said. "You're having a good time because the horses are all running well. It was great working there." Even though Stephens died in 1998, the bond remains. In the second race at Aqueduct, on December 10, 1999, Badgett sent out a first-time starter named Keep Ticking, a filly bred and owned by Lucille Stephens. Keep Ticking finished third in an encouraging debut.

Badgett picked up Christiana Stable less than two years after he went out on his own. Seth Hancock

advised him that he should expect a call. "And Rich Jones called me up and asked me if I'd be interested in training some horses for him," Badgett said.

Badgett didn't have to think twice. "An outfit like that, you have a chance to come up with a good horse," Badgett said.

Or a great one.

# CHAPTER 3

## A Beginning

With Henry Clark based solely in Maryland, Christiana Stables sent some of its horses to other trainers. Mrs. Lunger never regretted sending her New York string to Billy Badgett Jr. "He's a good, good man and a good horseman," she said.

Badgett had made a great first impression on Mrs. Lunger, but he certainly didn't sweep Rose Mundy off her feet.

Badgett laughs about it now. They never would have met without the assistance of Rose's friend, Sue Finley, a TV producer and publisher of the *Thoroughbred Daily News*. She is the wife of Bill Finley, the *New York Daily News* racing columnist. Sue, who at the time was working in the press office of the New York Racing Association, had spent one spring walking hots for Woody Stephens. "I had gotten to know Billy," Sue said.

"I was really bad at hotwalking and he would give me the easiest horses to walk. He's just a really nice guy."

So when *Daily News* photographer Daniel Farrell asked Sue for a favor, she thought of Billy Badgett. Farrell, a big horse racing fan, had been asked by another *Daily News* photographer, Rose's grandfather, Ed Clarity, if he knew anyone Rose could work for at the track to learn how to ride professionally. But there was a catch. Rose could only work until 9:30 every morning because she was going to college in Brooklyn at the time and had already planned on routinely taking weekends off to go skiing with her family. Sue called Badgett and relayed the request. "Billy said, 'This is a racetrack. She has to learn that you do what has to be done,' " Sue said. "He was tough on the phone."

Nevertheless, Sue took Rose to Badgett's barn. "Rose is beautiful, and Billy took one look at her and turned into a whole ball of mush," Sue said.

Badgett's recollection was a tad different:

"Sue and Rose came in my barn one day. I was actually back in a stall doing a horse up, and I'm looking out there, and Sue says, 'This is Rose, and she wants to learn how to ride. And I thought you'd be a good person for her.' I said, 'Look, I'm kind of busy right now. But okay, come back tomorrow.' "

Badgett gave Rose a job walking horses, but she made it known that she really wanted to ride. So Badgett let her get on the stable pony and gallop it around the track a few times. "And then I'd get on the pony," he said. "I'd put her on a horse and I started teaching her about being next to another horse. And one thing led to another and we started going out. Next thing you know, I'm getting married."

Actually, it was just a little bit more involved than that. And Rose's interest in horses was obviously genuine. Rose was born in Broad Channel in Queens, a tiny, mostly Catholic town on an island between Rockaway Beach and Howard Beach. Her dad, Dan Mundy, was a captain in the New York City Fire Department. Rose was one of five children, the one who always wanted a horse, even though she knew nothing of nearby Aqueduct.

She was nine when she began showing horses at her family's summer home in Prattsville in upstate New York. "My dad promised me that if I paid my own money, I could buy a horse," she said. So she got a paper route, delivering the *Daily News*. "It was a terrible job," she said. "I had a really big route, and I'd get five cent tips."

But she saved her money and did get a horse, Pebbles, when she was ten.

Rose was attending Kingsboro College in Brooklyn, studying liberal arts and trying to figure out what she was going to do with her life when her mom suggested she give the racetrack a try during summer vacation. "Like most people, as soon as I started going to the track, it got in my blood," Rose said.

She did confess to nagging her future husband relentlessly for an opportunity to ride. "Every day I begged and begged," she said. "Of course, I said I knew what I was doing because I used to show horses. Which didn't mean anything."

Actually, Rose was at a crossroads. She was working as a hotwalker for ninety-nine dollars a week, showing up each day at Belmont at 4 a.m. She would rush through her duties at the barn and hightail it to Brooklyn to make a 9:30 morning class. The strain was getting to her. She would fall asleep nights with a book in her hands and she was making little progress with Badgett about learning how to ride. "He said maybe I should go to South Carolina to learn how to ride," she said. "I didn't want to do that. But I was ready to go to an area farm to learn. Then he called me at home. I didn't even know if he had my home number. He said, 'Don't go anywhere. I need the help. I'll show you how to ride.' "

At the age of nineteen, fifteen years younger than Badgett, she found the two passions of her life: learning the intricacies of racing day by day by working with the man she would marry.

Although Badgett might have become smitten at this point, he demanded a lot from his would-be rider. In return, he taught her what she needed to know. Eventually, Rose got her wish and began exercising some of his horses.

Rose had an asset she had not yet discovered. She was a natural. She still is, so much so, that when Bevo won the 1999 Futurity at Belmont Park, rider Joe Bravo, who had never ridden the horse before, told a national television audience how Rose had counseled him before the race.

Rose had instructed Bravo to let the colt settle after the break. The first quarter mile, she told him, was the

crucial part of the race. If Bevo could settle and find his rhythm, he would give his all when it mattered. Bravo followed Rose's instructions with stellar results.

For his part, Badgett always heeds Rose's counsel when it comes to horses in the barn. He considers her an excellent rider with an instinctual feel for young horses: "The funny thing is that these two-year-olds come up here and I don't know who's going to be better than the other ones until they start breezing. But she always ends up on the good horse. It's amazing."

Rose's patience with young horses as she teaches them their early lessons is another asset, according to her husband. "And she's really, really good at breezing, phenomenal at breezing. If I tell her to go five-eighths in a minute, she's a fifth of a second on either side of that all the time. All the time. Which is a good person to have in your corner. That part of the game has gotten extremely difficult: breezing. It's just an art. Some people can do it; some people can't. There are guys galloping horses for twenty years that still can't breeze horses. So it's a big plus."

Christiana Stable shipped up its New York string from South Carolina to Belmont Park in April, 1989. By the summer, Badgett separated the precocious two-year-olds who would remain at Belmont Park and the others who would ship early to Saratoga for more seasoning. Go for Wand, who had missed some training because of a cough, didn't make the cut and left for Saratoga.

Although Go for Wand might have lacked precocity at that point, she stood out. Extremely attractive and big for her age, the filly also was sound and very correct. Rose took note of her "exceptional attitude."

Yet the filly's competitive fires had yet to be stoked. When Go for Wand began to breeze, she went along comfortably with the others, not yet ready to assert her superiority.

Rose, her regular rider, recalled how easily the filly performed her tasks: "She always breezed in hand."

Go for Wand also had a keen sense of curiosity. She liked to look at things, even if they scared her. On the racetrack, she would stand immobile at the eighth pole, looking around. But once it was time to go to work, Go for Wand was all business. "One minute, she was quiet, the next minute she was on the bit. Just smart," Rose said. "Even when she started getting tougher, she always checked: 'Should I switch my

lead? Can we go now?' Even in her breezes, she'd go :13 and :13. But you had to take a hold of her, and you had to stay calm. She was a good working filly. You had to work her. We didn't want to baby her."

Those mornings together, day after day, convinced Rose that Go for Wand had unusual talent. "It's not how fast they go; it's the way they hit the ground that's so different," she said. "There's something about the way that she hit the ground that felt much better. You can have your hands down on her withers and relax. And everything moves underneath you. You don't move. It's just a feeling that you can get. You just seem to be floating across the ground. I've had horses that I've liked, that have felt good, but hers seemed almost like a feminine way of moving. And then you'd see the other side of her, when you ask her and she just pours it on. And you know it's there. It's always there. And you're waiting for it."

Go for Wand didn't like waiting: for her carrots or for Rose's attention and affection. The two were so close that Rose could lie down in the filly's stall right next to her. Go for Wand would nuzzle her rider, searching for the carrot Rose always kept in her pocket. "She was feisty, but she would never touch me," Rose said. "She saw me coming, and she'd start pawing, and Billy would say, 'Go away, she's getting too excited. Leave her alone.'"

Go for Wand frequently took a different approach with Badgett. She tried to bite him. Although Badgett appreciated the special bond between Rose and the filly, it sometimes made him impatient — especially when Go for Wand's would stand at the eighth pole. "I used to get mad at her: 'Come on, let's go!,' " he said.

Badgett did have business to attend to with Go for Wand, even though he was about as far away from being pressured to race his two-year-olds as possible.

Mrs. Lunger didn't like two-year-old racing, and as a result Christiana seldom hurried its youngsters. But Badgett tried to persuade his owner that Go for Wand was special.

Christiana had had prior success with two-year-olds, winning the Futurity with both Cyane in 1961 and his son, Salem, nine years later. A filly named Unity Hall won a stakes at Belmont in early summer, but by that fall, she had lost her form. Unity Hall produced Linkage, who didn't run until late in his two-year-old year, and several other stakes horses. Unity Hall's loss of form "contributed to a mindset that these horses needed more time," Richard Jones said.

Go for Wand got that time, and by mid-summer was nearing her debut. "We could have run her at Saratoga, but we elected to give her a little more chance to grow and fill out," Badgett said.

But she did work seriously at Saratoga. And she got a jockey. All on the same morning.

# CHAPTER 4

## *A Profile In Courage*

Randy Romero seemed born into race riding in Louisiana. "To this day, it's all I know," he said.

Born on December, 22, 1957, Romero was raised on his family's farm in Erath, twenty miles outside of Lafayette. Though his dad, Lloyd, was a policeman, his grandfather, Henry, was a farmer and trapper, and Randy, the middle son of five boys, spent his childhood with horses. Racing them. Randy was riding on the bush tracks populating Louisiana when he was eight years old. "We used to bet with the spending money, with our allowance," he said. "Twenty-five or thirty cents."

In 1975, Randy rode Rocket's Magic, a Quarter Horse trained by Lloyd Romero, to a third-place finish in the All American Futurity at Ruidoso Downs in New Mexico. In the movie *Casey's Shadow,* which was based loosely on the Romero family, the horse wins the race.

By age eighteen, Randy Romero was riding his first Thoroughbreds at Evangeline Downs in Lafayette, Louisiana. There, he met his future wife, Cricket, the daughter of a trainer. They were still teenagers when they married.

In 1979, Romero ventured to Fair Grounds in New Orleans, intent upon making a name for himself. His enthusiasm was as unbridled as his talent. "I just had the drive to do it," he said. "I was around the horses so much. I've always been good. I'm lucky to say that."

"Luck" and Romero don't belong in the same sentence. For while his career rocketed to the top of his profession — he became leading rider at Evangeline Downs as a seventeen-year-old apprentice and emerged as one of the greatest riders ever — he has endured more pain than any person should ever have to endure. "When I was young, I was really tough," he said. "I was brought up tough." He spent his entire career proving that. Over and over and over.

By the age of twenty-five, he had already graduated from the smaller tracks of Louisiana, winning jockey titles at Evangeline Downs, Delta Downs, and Jefferson Downs, to ride at Oaklawn Park and Fair Grounds. On an otherwise nondescript day in 1983, he was sitting in the hot box in the jockey's room at Oaklawn Park trying to lose a couple pounds. A light bulb exploded, igniting the rubbing alcohol covering his body. His body was burned so severely — second and third degree burns over sixty percent of his body — that doctors gave him a forty percent chance to live. He was back riding in fifteen weeks.

"I was very fortunate that it wasn't my time to go," Romero said in April, 2000. "I had a lot of people beside me. I had a lot of support, my wife Cricket, and my son, Randy II (then three). I had something to live for. I wouldn't let myself go down. I'm a survivor."

Twenty-two more conventional accidents, twenty-one operations, and sixteen fractures were the price Romero paid to reach the top of his profession, which he clearly did after moving to New York in 1986, and attempting to get back to that lofty level after he fell with Go for Wand in the 1990 Breeders' Cup. He retired in July, 1999, at the age of forty-one to become a jockey's agent for Marlon St. Julien, also from Louisiana.

"Randy's had a tough life," Badgett said. "Most jocks

in his case would have retired earlier. The guy's just lived through pain his whole life."

At times, it seemed worth it. Romero rode the undefeated filly Personal Ensign to a thirteen-for-thirteen record, capping her career with a nose victory over Kentucky Derby winner Winning Colors in the 1988 Breeders' Cup Distaff at Churchill Downs.

The following summer, Romero got on an unraced two-year-old filly named Go for Wand for a workout. He would end 1989 thirteenth in the country in earnings with more than $6.6 million and tied for thirteenth in victories with 266. He already had climbed to thirty-third in all-time victories (3,517) in sixteen seasons, fewer years riding than all but one of the thirty-two jockeys ahead of him, Chris McCarron, who had won 5,103 races in fifteen years. Romero finished his career with 4,294 wins, three Breeders' Cup victories and riding titles at ten different tracks.

"He probably looked terrible on a horse, but horses just ran for him," Badgett said. "Probably because he had a tremendous attitude as far as being happy-go-lucky. Nothing ever bothered him, nothing. You can see a lot of people just getting down and affected by things that happen to them every day on a daily basis. But he never got that. He was always upbeat and happy. He loved his work. He loved his horses."

And on an August morning of the third week at Saratoga in 1989, Romero, for once in his life, got lucky. Go for Wand was nearing her debut, and Romero happened to be at the Badgett barn when she was ready for a serious five furlong work. Badgett asked Romero if he'd breeze the filly and she worked superbly. "She was right on top of running, and she went five-eighths in like :59, as easy as a horse can go :59," Badgett said.

Badgett had a problem, but it was a good one: calming Romero down after the workout. "She was so strong," Romero said. "You could tell she was naturally gifted. She was that special one. I said, 'Billy, if she stays sound, she'll win the Breeders' Cup.' He said, 'Don't be telling that to nobody.' "

Badgett admonished Romero to keep his excitement to himself. What if Romero were wrong? What if the filly didn't fulfill expectations? It was better, the trainer figured, just to take things one day at a time.

Romero calmed down, then said, "I'd really like to

ride her." Badgett replied, "She's yours, Randy," even though his regular riders at the time were Jerry Bailey and Mike Smith. "Randy was just in the right place at the right time," Badgett said. "And I'm kind of a loyal person as far as that goes. He was so pumped up about her, I couldn't let somebody else ride her in her maiden race."

No other jockey ever rode her in any race. "There were a lot of riders trying to take her away from me, but Billy was a man of his word," Romero said. "He was loyal. I thank him so much for what he did. There are a lot of people who wouldn't have. He's loyal, and he's a friend."

Badgett could have raced Go for Wand at Saratoga, for she was blossoming and training superbly. Everything came so easily to her. However, the trainer opted to wait and run her at Belmont.

The word was out. Go for Wand went off the 2-1 second choice from the six post in a field of nine in her career debut, September 14 at Belmont Park, even though she happened to catch a field which would prove to be star-studded. "It was just one of those races," Billy said. "You don't know anything about the horses; they're all first-time starters. But it turned out three graded stakes winners came out of that same race, a phenomenal maiden race."

Go for Wand dusted them. Third by three lengths after a quarter mile, she won by four lengths in 1:10 3/5, a scintillating six-furlong performance for a first-time starter. Nina was second and future graded stakes winners Worth Avenue and Seaside Attraction were third and fourth, respectively. Go for Wand's debut was an appetizer. Disdaining a stakes race, Badgett entered her in a one mile allowance race October 2 at Belmont. It rained. Go for Wand won by eighteen and a quarter lengths as the 3-2 favorite on a sloppy track, getting a mile in 1:36 3/5 with a final quarter in :24 4/5. "She just exploded," Romero said. "I knew that day she was something that doesn't come around every day."

Mrs. Lunger had to take his word for it. She missed both of Go for Wand's first two races. "The first time she ran, my daughter and I were going to New York to watch, when we were caught in a vast accident on the bridge," Mrs. Lunger told Lucy Acton in a story in the January, 1990 issue of *Maryland Horse*. "A crane had fallen. There was no way we could make it there on time. The second time she ran, I was away, accompa-

nying my grandson to the University of St. Andrews in Scotland. We were in a vessel crossing the Atlantic."

But the entire family was on hand to see Go for Wand run in the Frizette Stakes.

Go for Wand

# CHAPTER 5

## *Stakes Time*

There is nothing giddier in horse racing than owning a two-year-old who has yet to be tested. Nobody knows how much talent the horse has. Nobody knows the limits. Nobody even knows if there are limits.

After watching Go for Wand win her first two starts by four and eighteen and a quarter lengths, respectively, Badgett knew it was time to find out. He chose the grade I Frizette Stakes at Belmont Park on October 14, just twelve days after her second start. Trainer D. Wayne Lukas picked the same race for Peter Brant's more seasoned two-year-old filly Stella Madrid, who was seeking her third consecutive grade I stakes win after taking the Spinaway Stakes at Saratoga by four and a half lengths and the Matron at Belmont by two and three-quarters lengths. She was ridden by Angel Cordero Jr. Another contender, Dance Colony, entered the Frizette undefeated in four starts. But such was the quality of Go for Wand's first two races that she was made the even-money favorite. Stella Madrid was 3-2 and Dance Colony 3-1 in the field of seven two-year-old fillies racing one mile.

Badgett was concerned about the lack of moisture in the track. It hadn't rained for some time, and the track was loose and cuppy: "If there was one thing Go for Wand didn't like, it was that. And then the only other time she really caught that kind of racetrack was at Churchill Downs on the day of the Kentucky Oaks."

They were the only two races she lost before the 1990 Breeders' Cup.

In the 1989 Frizette, Stella Madrid delivered a superior performance, overcoming a poor start to take a two-length lead to the sixteenth pole. Go for Wand had prompted the pace in second throughout, but a half-length deficit after the first quarter had increased to a length after a half-mile, to two lengths after three-quarters, and to two and a half lengths in early stretch before Go for Wand kicked in again. She closed the gap between them quickly. Now Stella Madrid's lead was a length and a half, then a length, then three-quarters of a length. The two hit the wire, Stella Madrid a half-length in front.

The final time for the mile in the Frizette was 1:38 4/5, with a final quarter run in a pedestrian :27 4/5. Still, Go for Wand had beaten third-place finisher Dance Colony by five and a quarter lengths.

Although Badgett was disappointed Go for Wand lost, he was pleased with the way she responded when Romero asked her to run. The jockey had no doubt Go for Wand would vanquish the winner in their next match-up.

The next race was the $1-million Breeders' Cup Juvenile Fillies at Gulfstream Park in Florida. Go for Wand would face Stella Madrid again, as well as another Lukas stablemate, Eugene Klein's Special Happening, the winner of the grade II, $217,500 Alcibiades Stakes at Keeneland, her second victory in three starts. Dance Colony would be there, as well as Sweet Roberta, a ten-length winner of the grade II Selima Stakes at Laurel, and Trumpet's Blare, a five-length winner of the grade I Arlington-Washington Lassie Stakes. A field of twelve would go postward in the Juvenile Fillies on November 4, 1989.

Badgett drew on a lesson from Woody Stephens: when shipping a horse to a different climate, do it either three weeks early or just a day or two before. "Shipping from the cold to the hot weather, the acclimation is very important," Badgett explained. "If you ship a couple days before the race, the adrenaline is still flowing and they're okay. If you ship three weeks early, they can adjust. But if you ship nine or ten days before, they let down."

Badgett chose three weeks and, the day before the Breeders' Cup, he told reporters he was happy he did: "I'm really glad I brought her down here when I did. The first couple of days she dropped her head a little bit, but now she's fine."

The three weeks gave Badgett and Rose a lot of free time. They only had one horse at Gulfstream, so they could go to the beach in the mornings, then return to the barn so Rose could walk Go for Wand in the afternoons. After dinner, they would check on her again. "It really started to be a joke," Rose said. "She knew the sound of the car. Billy used to yell at me, 'Don't go near her,' at night because she'd get so excited to see me."

Romero fought over-confidence. "I didn't think I'd

lose," he said. "I had just that much confidence in her. I knew the horse to beat was Stella Madrid. I knew if I could stay out of trouble, I could. I rode her with all the confidence in the world."

Badgett was confident, too. Then, roughly two hours before the first Breeders' Cup race, the Sprint, it rained. For fifteen minutes. "She was a superior mudder," Badgett said. "Whenever it got wet, I'll tell you, it was scary what she could do. She just excelled in the mud. And it just poured down rain and the track got a lot of moisture in it. I'm saying to myself, 'I can't believe this.' I was hoping it would rain more, but it got enough moisture in the track where it did certainly help her."

The track would be rated fast. So would Badgett and Rose's filly.

Rose jogged Go for Wand one and a half times around the track at 5:30 the morning of the Breeders' Cup. After they got back to the barn, Go for Wand began searching. "She was looking for carrots," Rose said. "But she didn't get any. Not on race day."

Eight hours later, Rose walked Go for Wand onto the track for the Breeders' Cup Juvenile Fillies. Badgett walked ten yards away by himself.

Go for Wand had drawn the four post; Stella Madrid the five. Stella Madrid went off the 2-1 favorite; Go for Wand 5-2, which was the highest odds she would ever go off at, Trumpet's Blare 4-1, and Sweet Roberta 9-2. The other eight fillies were double-digit odds.

Upstairs, Rose took her seat directly in front of Mrs. Lunger, an arrangement Mrs. Lunger would subsequently insist upon. When the starting gate opened, Mrs. Lunger gently patted Rose on her back, which would also become another ritual for good luck. Badgett watched the race from near the winner's circle.

Chris McCarron put Special Happening on the lead immediately, while Romero tucked Go for Wand in neatly on the rail, alternating fifth and sixth. Heading into the far turn, Stella Madrid went after her uncoupled stablemate on the lead while Go for Wand split horses decisively and moved into third. Stella Madrid had to work hard to get past Special Happening, and when she did Go for Wand pounced on her. Under eight right-handed taps with the whip, Go for Wand surged past as Badgett screamed, "Hang on there, Randy! Hang on there, Randy!" Rose yelled, "Mrs. Lunger, she's going to do it! She's going to win!"

Announcer Tom Durkin called the finish: "She's going to win it. She's going to win it going away."

Rose said, "We were jumping up and down, hugging everybody. I remember trembling. And right away, people led us to the winner's circle." Which was crowded when they arrived. Rose, who would have preferred a private moment with her filly, patted Wanda on her neck and told her, "I'm so proud."

Go for Wand had won by two and three-quarters lengths, the largest margin of the seven Breeders' Cup championship races that day, getting a mile and a sixteenth in 1:44 1/5, three-fifths of a second slower than Rhythm's winning time later in the day in the Breeders' Cup Juvenile. Sweet Roberta got up for second, a half-length ahead of Stella Madrid.

"It was the ultimate," Romero said. "I said, 'I got me another monster.' I was so fortunate to be a part of it. It was overwhelming. This is what you work all your life for, to get this type, and I got two of them. In two years time, I rode the two best fillies in the world."

For Badgett, the excitement gave him such a rush that when all the fanfare finally subsided, he felt mentally drained.

Go for Wand's effort earned her the Eclipse Award for champion two-year-old filly. Who knew how good she would be at three? She had just won the Breeders' Cup without even changing leads, becoming Christiana Stable's twenty-fifth homebred to win a stakes.

Go for Wand was not the only impressive winner that day. Noted Turf writer John Pricci wrote in his Breeders' Cup story in *Newsday* the next day, "Septuagenarian owner Mrs. Harry Lunger charmed all with her sense of humor, something of a rarity at this level in the sport."

# CHAPTER 6

## *Transition*

While there was some speculation in the media about Go for Wand needing to win the Demoiselle Stakes after the Breeders' Cup to clinch a championship, Badgett and Mrs. Lunger never gave it a thought, and Go for Wand was voted the Eclipse champion anyway. Accordingly, The Jockey Club Committee of Tommy Trotter, Bruce Lombardi, and Howard Battle rated Go for Wand the experimental high-weight three-year-old filly for 1990 at 123 pounds. Stella Madrid was rated second at 121.

Two days after the Breeders' Cup, Go for Wand was sent to Camden, South Carolina, to be reunited with Jamie Woodington. Badgett went to see her in December and also to look in on some Christiana yearlings.

Since the Breeders' Cup, Go for Wand had grown and put on about 100 pounds. But she still had a little more growing to do. "You always hope they can make the transition from two to three," Badgett said, "and she did that unbelievably well."

Badgett, then wintering in Florida, made another visit in early February. What he saw pleased him. Go for Wand had matured even more. That was important, as she would be tested with a demanding stakes schedule. "I put her through probably one of the most rigorous campaigns you can put a three-year-old filly through, only because she seemed to come out of each race as good as she went into it," Badgett said.

The trainer had carefully considered her 1990 schedule. The early season goal was the Kentucky Oaks; the summer goal the Alabama and, of course, the final goal was the Breeders' Cup at Belmont Park, where Go for Wand would enjoy home field advantage.

Go for Wand was not the only one going through a transition. Rose and Billy's relationship had obviously changed, too, and their engagement and wedding roughly coincided, respectively, with the 1989 and 1990 Breeders' Cups.

Rose worked for Badgett for almost a year before the two started to date. But first they were friends, going out to lunch and talking horses. Then Rose started to ride. "Then we started dating over the winter," she said. "We lived together for quite a while before we were engaged before the 1989 Breeders' Cup."

They were wed in Howard Beach in Queens on October 6, 1990, the day before Go for Wand won the Beldame Stakes in an overpowering performance. "We didn't go on a honeymoon," she said. "We put that off because the Breeders' Cup was coming. We were going away four days later. And that was the Breeders' Cup that she..." Rose's voice softened to a whisper, "Was put down, got hurt."

Badgett chose the seven-furlong Beaumont Stakes at Keeneland for Go for Wand's three-year-old debut on April 10, 1990. "She trained awfully good," Badgett said. "She worked three-quarters in 1:10 2/5 six days from the race. I thought it might have been a little too fast, but she had done that before. She did it so easy. She got back to the barn. She ate up good."

Six days later, she devoured the competition. In a field of six on a muddy track, Go for Wand won by eight and a half lengths in 1:26 2/5, breaking On to Royalty's 1988 stakes record by a fifth of a second.

Trumpet's Blare was second, a head in front of Seaside Attraction. "Any time you win a championship, winning the first race back is always a lot of weight off your shoulders," Badgett said.

The fifty-third running of the $224,100 grade I Ashland Stakes at Keeneland was next, just eleven days later, and Go for Wand would have a new challenger. Her name was Charon. Owned by Stanley M. Ersoff and trained by seventy-five-year-old Eugene Navarro, Charon had won all four of her starts, two as a two-year-old at Calder and then two more at three when she stepped up considerably in competition to a pair of graded stakes at Gulfstream Park. In her three-year-old debut in the grade III Forward Gal Stakes on February 14, Charon beat Trumpet's Blare by two and a quarter lengths. In the grade II Bonnie Miss Stakes on March 11, Charon was sent off the third choice against Trumpet's Blare and De La Devil, who had finished third in the Forward Gal. The result was the same. Charon won by two lengths over Trumpet's Blare, with De La Devil a neck back in third.

In an interview in the *Lexington Herald-Leader* four days before the Ashland, Navarro told writer Christy

McIntyre that he was looking forward to the meeting with Go for Wand. "She's a runner," Navarro said. "All I can say is I'm glad to run with her. If I finish behind her, it would be a good race. If I happen to beat her, I'd say we have something special here."

Bettors in the crowd of 24,083 at Keeneland demurred, making Go for Wand the 3-10 favorite in a field reduced to five when Seaside Attraction scratched. Charon was the 3-1 second choice in the mile and a sixteenth race, and Trumpet's Blare was third choice at nearly 7-1. Joyce Azalene was 22-1 and Piper Piper, a maiden, 30-1. The drying out track was rated "muddy." Go for Wand breezed.

With Seaside Attraction out, Joyce Azalene set the pace and dawdled through a first quarter in :24 3/5 with Charon second under Earlie Fires and Go for Wand three-wide in third. As the slow pace continued, Go for Wand could wait no longer and took Romero to the lead past the half in :48 2/5. Charon took over second and tried to keep up, but could not as Go for Wand coasted home five lengths in front. Charon was second, seven and a half lengths in front of Piper Piper. Joyce Azalene was another eight lengths back in fourth.

Trumpet's Blare had been pulled up on the first turn by jockey Craig Perret after possibly suffering a pinched nerve. Go for Wand's winning time of 1:43 3/5 was just two-fifths of a second off Gorgeous' 1989 stakes record.

And Go for Wand had switched leads. "She switched leads in just one of her other races, when she won by eighteen and a quarter in the mud," Badgett told reporters afterwards. "It never bothered me. She won the Breeders' Cup without switching leads."

Navarro was impressed. "Oh my god, she's terrific," he said. "She's one of the best fillies I've seen in a long, long time."

Romero, who won five races that day, said, "She was just pulling me out of the saddle, and she was going easy. She's going to be something great. She's something special."

Her Ashland performance raised the question: Could she beat colts? It went unanswered. Go for Wand would not enter the Kentucky Derby, even though a filly, Winning Colors, had won the classic two years earlier. "Mrs. Lunger is dead set against running fillies against colts this time of the year, so we didn't even nominate her to the Triple Crown," Badgett told reporters.

Could another three-year-old filly beat her? "I wouldn't say she's unbeatable, but she's going to be very tough to beat," Badgett said. Her competition would get its next chance in the Kentucky Oaks. Badgett and Mrs. Lunger had opted for the filly classic at Churchill Downs on May 4th over the Acorn Stakes, the first leg of the Triple Tiara, at Belmont Park on May 26th. "If I had to do it all over again, I might have gotten her up to Belmont and run in the Triple Tiara," he said.

Then he explained why he would have bypassed the Kentucky Oaks: "There was nothing wrong with the racetrack, but it just hadn't gotten any water on it. She had an excellent work at Churchill when the track was fast, but then it rained. They sealed it and it became a different ballgame. Churchill Downs can be a very funny racetrack anyway. Either they love it or they don't. She didn't like it. Probably, if I had to do it all over again, I might not have run her."

There was another factor weighing on his mind. "Not too often are you going to get a horse to go in the Beaumont at seven-eighths and come back and go in the Ashland and then go back in the Kentucky Oaks,"

he said. "Your normal horse, you'd be asking an extreme lot, but I knew also that she wasn't catching extreme competition, so the races were a little bit easier on her. If she had had to run hard to do something, it might have been a different story."

The story unfolded in front of a crowd of 67,483 on hand to see the 116th Kentucky Oaks. When the track came up muddy, Go for Wand appeared even more invincible and went off at odds of 1-5. "If you'd polled the media or all the trainers on the backside when it started to rain today, everybody would have said there's no way this filly can get beat," trainer D. Wayne Lukas said.

It didn't stop Lukas from saddling three of the four fillies he had entered in the Oaks: Seaside Attraction, Bright Candles, who was second in the Santa Anita Oaks, and allowance winner Paper Money. William Young's Overbrook Farm was the sole owner of Seaside Attraction and co-owner with Lukas of the other two. Lukas scratched his other filly, Santa Anita Oaks winner Hail Atlantis. "I remember seeing the jockeys coming into the paddock, three of them wearing our good friend Bill Young's silks," Richard Jones said. "That was the first time I thought of horse racing as a team sport."

It took only one to upset Go for Wand: Seaside Attraction, a $1.05 million weanling by Seattle Slew. In the Beaumont, Seaside Attraction hit her head on the starting gate and recovered to finish third, eight and a half lengths behind Go for Wand. Lukas scratched Seaside Attraction from the Ashland, ironically, because the track was muddy. Seaside Attraction relished the muddy track at Churchill Downs, stalking stablemate Bright Candles through a slow first quarter of :24 and taking command before the half in :48 1/5. She then posted splits of 1:13 and 1:39 under Chris McCarron before getting the nine furlongs in 1:52 4/5, three lengths ahead of Go for Wand, who held second by three lengths over Bright Candles.

It hadn't taken Romero long to realize his filly was struggling. "She wasn't comfortable," he said. "Usually, she's in the bit the whole time, but she fought me today. Six jumps out of the gate, I knew she was having trouble."

Jones said, "It was very disappointing because she was the horse of a lifetime. She looked invincible."

Badgett was initially disappointed, too. Then he

**Go for Wand, shown winning the 1990 Mother Goose Stakes at Belmont Park, "knew she was special," according to those closest to her.**

**Obeah (left) was twenty-two when she produced Go for Wand from a mating to champion Deputy Minister (top left). The stakes-winning Obeah was a daughter of Christiana star Cyane (top), while Deputy Minister was sired by Northern Dancer's son Vice Regent (above).**

Jane Lunger (right) founded Christiana Stable with her late husband Harry soon after Delaware Park opened in 1937. In a 1947 winner's circle presentation, Mrs. Lunger (far right) is shown with her husband (far left), and with trainer Billy Badgett and jockey Randy Romero (top) in 1990 after Go for Wand's Ashland Stakes victory.

Billy Badgett served his apprenticeship under Hall of Fame trainer Woody Stephens. He and his wife, Rose, who was Go for Wand's exercise rider, pose with their star before the 1990 Breeders' Cup.

Rose Badgett and Go for Wand shared a special bond. The two were so close that Rose could lie down in the filly's stall right next to her. Go for Wand would nuzzle her rider, searching for the carrot Rose always kept in her pocket.

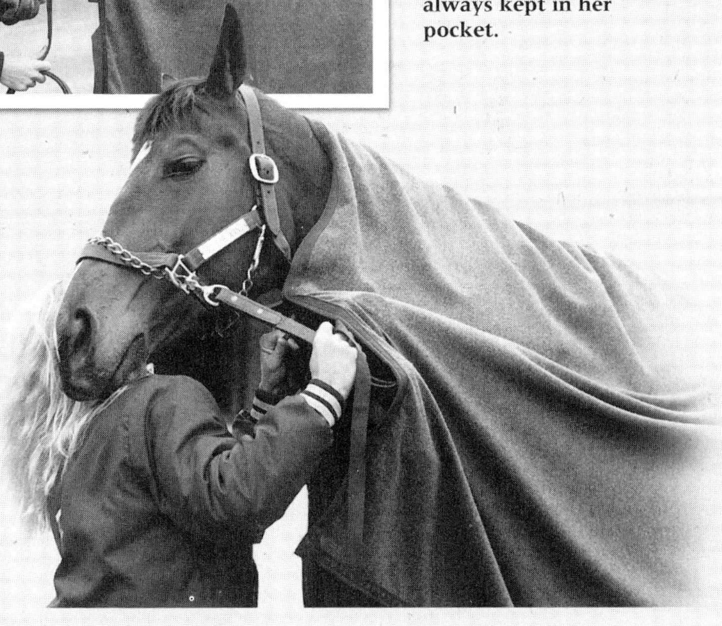

**Randy Romero got his start at Evangeline Downs in Louisiana. He rose to the highest levels of the sport while suffering a staggering number of injuries. Shown in a winner's circle presentation early in his career (right) and signing autographs at Evangeline Downs after riding his last race, on July 19, 1999.**

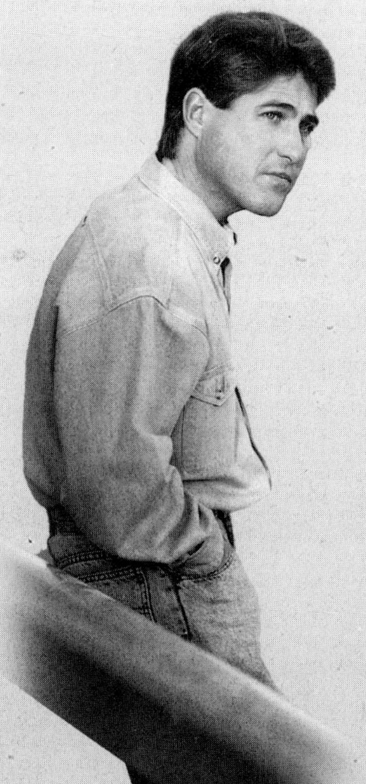

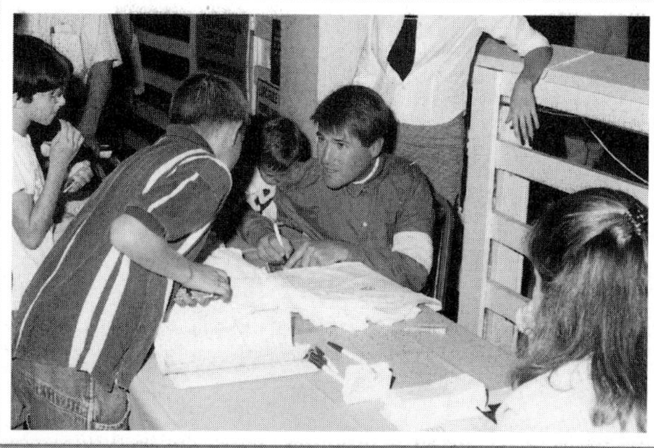

Go for Wand was outrun by Stella Madrid (above) in the 1989 Frizette, but rebounded to defeat a top field in that year's Breeders' Cup Juvenile Fillies at Gulfstream Park (top).

Go for Wand's Juvenile Fillies victory made her three-for-four in her first year of racing, and secured the first of two eventual Eclipse Awards.

Go for Wand began her three-year-old campaign with a victory in Keeneland's Beaumont Stakes (right), then scored impressively in the Ashland Stakes (above). On her way to the post (below) for the Ashland.

**Go for Wand struggled in the Kentucky Oaks and lost to Seaside Attraction (top left), then returned to Belmont Park to score emphatically in the Mother Goose.**

**Go for Wand gave her all in the mornings, as well as on raceday afternoons. In the Test (above), she equaled the stakes record.**

In the Alabama (above), Go for Wand broke the stakes record in defeating Charon by seven lengths. Randy Romero signals her supremacy after the race.

Go for Wand usually won by so much that Romero had to look back for her closest competitor. In the Maskette (above) at Belmont, the filly cruised home a professional two and a half lengths ahead of Feel the Beat. The Maskette was later renamed for Go for Wand and moved to Saratoga.

In the Beldame, Go for Wand defeated her elders in stakes-record time. Afterward, her connections paid homage at the barn.

Go for Wand had the measure of Bayakoa in the 1990 Breeders' Cup Distaff until her fall in mid-stretch.

Go for Wand is buried at Saratoga, site of some of her greatest victories.

remembered all the other good horses who had gotten beat on that track. Go for Wand ran as hard as she could. That was all Badgett, or anyone, could expect.

Time offers perspective. Running second by three lengths in a ten-horse field in a grade I stakes turned out to be the poorest performance of her career, a performance other horsemen would snatch in a second. But she was never just another horse.

# CHAPTER 7

## *Vindication — And Then Some*

The late spring of 1990 was awfully kind to Billy Badgett. First, he was named New York trainer of the famed Greentree Stable. Next, his long-time friend Seth Hancock sent him some of Claiborne Farm's best two-year-olds. In an interview with the *Daily Racing Form*'s Mike Watchmaker, Badgett said, "I pinch myself every once in a while to make sure I'm not dreaming, especially because of Go for Wand. I wake up in the morning and go to her stall, and sometimes I can't believe I'm actually training a horse like her."

He was, and now she was coming off a surprisingly lackluster second in the Kentucky Oaks. Who could blame Charon's trainer, Eugene Navarro, for taking another shot at her in the Mother Goose? After running second by five lengths to Go for Wand in the Ashland, Charon had delivered a devastating performance in the grade II Black-Eyed Susan at Pimlico, winning by seven and a quarter lengths. D. Wayne Lukas entered two of his string of stakes fillies, Stella Madrid, who was five-for-five at Belmont Park after taking the Acorn, and Bright Candles, who was third in both the Kentucky Oaks and Black-Eyed Susan. Only two other fillies entered the mile and an eighth Mother Goose: Danzig's Beauty and Dance Colony. Despite the others' considerable credentials and her loss in Kentucky, Go for Wand went off the 4-5 favorite breaking from the outside post in the field of six.

Stella Madrid set the pace while Romero kept Go for Wand in a close stalking position, first three-wide on the backstretch and then two wide as Danzig's Beauty could not keep up through a quarter in :23 1/5 and a half in :46. Go for Wand moved to Stella Madrid's flank and stuck there as Charon moved up a closer third heading into the far turn. Stella Madrid still held the lead heading toward the stretch, and her jockey, Cordero, tried floating Go for Wand and Charon wide, but both of them rolled past. Romero tapped Go for Wand six times right-handed, twice left-handed, and four more times right-handed after she opened a clear lead of maybe two lengths and Charon tried to close in. Romero looked back over his right shoulder to make sure he had Charon safe and let Go for Wand coast home a length and a quarter winner. Charon held second, four and a quarter lengths ahead of Stella Madrid.

Romero was not surprised with Go for Wand's triumphant return to New York. "I had no questions or doubts about her," he said after the Mother Goose. "I know what kind of mare she is. She's a super mare. Billy has done a great job with her. All I did was steer her. I can't take any of the credit."

Navarro was philosophical after watching Charon's lifetime record drop to five wins and two seconds in seven starts, both losses to Go for Wand. "Mine's a good filly, but the other filly was better," he said. "Charon might get better. So we'll try Go for Wand again."

That was scheduled to be in the Coaching Club American Oaks, but Go for Wand never made it, getting a cough after the Mother Goose. "I thought she'd get over it quicker than she did, but it lingered on for a couple of weeks," Badgett told Mike Veitch, racing writer for the *Saratogian*. "I had to walk her for about

ten days. I possibly could have made the Coaching Club American Oaks, but it would have been asking a lot. That would have been putting an awful lot of pressure on her."

With the grade I Alabama at Saratoga a stakes dear to Mrs. Lunger's heart — having won the 1982 Alabama with Broom Dance, a daughter of Dance Spell — Badgett pointed Go for Wand to the grade I, $122,400 Test Stakes there nine days earlier.

Without her nemesis, Charon romped in the Coaching Club by nine lengths. Charon's next start would be in the Alabama, but Go for Wand still had a difficult assignment in the Test, and Badgett was realistic about the hurdle of a fifty-three-day layoff heading into a seven-furlong sprint. "I told Mrs. Lunger that if she got beat, don't worry about it, because this was not our main objective," Badgett said. "I just wanted a good race over the track, and I didn't want it to be that hard."

But it was. And it was even harder on the nine three-year-old fillies who opposed her.

The opposition included Stella Madrid, just one of two fillies ever to beat her; Screen Prospect, who had won the La Troienne Stakes at Churchill Downs;

California speedball Forest Fealty, the winner of the grade III, seven-furlong Railbird Stakes at Hollywood Park in a quick 1:21 3/5, and Token Dance, a two-length winner of the grade II Prioress Stakes at Belmont.

Go for Wand had trained superbly. She worked six furlongs in 1:13 1/5 at Belmont on July 18; five furlongs on a muddy track at Belmont in 1:01 1/5 on July 23, and a bullet five furlongs at Saratoga in :59 2/5 on July 29, four days before the Test.

Go for Wand was the 6-5 favorite in the field of ten in the sixty-fifth running of the grade I Test Stakes on August 2. She drew the two post. Stella Madrid was the 7-2 second choice breaking from the rail under Cordero. Screen Prospect and Craig Perret were 9-2 from the four post; Forest Fealty 5-1 with Julio Garcia from the eight post and Token Dance 8-1 under Eddie Maple from the six. Forest Fealty broke superbly, so fast that she got the jump on Stella Madrid. Go for Wand broke eighth, then was ninth for a second before she dragged Randy Romero along a clear path on the inside to engage Forest Fealty at the quarter in :22 1/5.

"They just out-footed her," Romero said. "They were too quick for her early. I wasn't concerned. I rode

her like she was unbeatable. Every time I rode her, I made sure there wasn't a straw in her path, because when I did call on her, she would always accelerate. That day, she exploded. I wasn't going to fight her and mess up her stride."

Go for Wand battled Forest Fealty head to head through a half in :44 3/5 as Stella Madrid struggled to stay with them. She couldn't. Go for Wand took the lead by a head, but Forest Fealty countered to regain the lead by a nose midway on the turn. That didn't sit well with Go for Wand, who quickly countered again and put Forest Fealty away, opening a length and a half lead.

Then the rest of the field swarmed in. Token Dance had rallied strongly on the inside, and Maple took her three-wide off the turn for a clear shot at the leader. Behind her, Screen Prospect was quickly gaining momentum.

They reached the eighth pole in an incredible 1:08 1/5, just one-fifth of a second off Spanish Riddle's 1972 record (which still stood through 1999), and Go for Wand was still strong. She crossed the wire two lengths in front of Screen Prospect in 1:21, matching Very Subtle's 1987 stakes record, just three-fifths of a second off Darby Creek Road's 1978 track record of 1:20 2/5 (which also is still standing through 1999).

"I kind of urged her to finish up," Romero said. "She had some other races coming up, but she was always within herself."

This was a tune up?

"She's unbelievable," Badgett said after the race. "When I saw :44 and change, I was surprised that she was laying that close. She just dragged Randy to the lead."

With a three-year-old colt division lacking a clear leader, the question was asked of Badgett if he would run in the Travers instead of the Alabama. "Mrs. Lunger really wants to win the Alabama more than anything else, so we haven't contemplated the Travers," Badgett said at the time.

In 1999, he sounded like he had contemplated it very seriously. "I was extremely, extremely tempted to try the Travers, just because I thought they were a very mediocre group of colts," Badgett said. "Actually, she ran two seconds faster in the Alabama than they did in the Travers (Rhythm's time on a fast track was 1 4/5 seconds slower). She could have won that race."

Go for Wand had reached a new level of performance in the Test, so much so that trainer Peter Vestal was delighted that his Screen Prospect had finished second. "She ran the race of her life," he said. "She got beat by the best three-year-old filly in America. The time is fantastic. She ran a heck of a race. I'm proud of her."

Regardless, one trainer wanted another shot at Go for Wand, Eugene Navarro. He believed that if his filly Charon would ever beat her, it would be in the 110th running of the mile and a quarter Alabama. Only one other three-year-old filly entered the race, Pampered Star, who had just won the grade II Monmouth Oaks by two and three-quarters lengths for trainer Bobby Frankel. A fourth filly would have earned $13,056, but when there were no takers, the money reverted back to the New York Racing Association, which banned place, show, and exacta wagering for the three-horse race. The connections of Crowned and Dance Colony, who had been contemplating the Alabama, decided their horses had seen enough of Go for Wand and skipped the race, which turned out to be more of a coronation than a contest.

[To ride Go for Wand that day, Romero gave up the mount on Hansel, a promising two-year-old trained by Frank Brothers who'd given Romero his second of three consecutive Tremont Stakes victories at Belmont Park. "There was a conflict," Romero said. "Hansel was in the Sapling (at Monmouth) and Go for Wand was in the Alabama. I told Frankie Brothers, I didn't think he wouldn't win the Sapling, but I wanted to be with her. Hansel, I always thought he was a special horse. Later, I was going to get back on him, and I broke my elbow, before the Jim Beam. (Jerry) Bailey got on him and stayed on him." Hansel went on to win the 1991 Preakness and Belmont Stakes under Bailey.]

But Romero's choice had nothing to do with sentiment, more about faith. "I believed in her," he said. "I thought she was a super nice filly."

Pampered Star drew the rail, Charon to her right and Go for Wand in the three post, sent off at odds of 9-2, 3-2, and 1-2, respectively, by a crowd of 32,480. Two and a half inches of rain the previous night had left a track rated "muddy" for the first race before it was upgraded to "good" by the Alabama.

The three fillies broke together, but Go for Wand

quickly made the lead as Perret on Charon took a stalking position to her immediate outside. Pampered Star was never in the race and was eased.

With Romero sitting motionless, Go for Wand set all the fractions as Perret kept his filly close, alternating between three-quarters of a length to a length and a quarter behind. Several times Charon moved closer to Go for Wand, but as the horses headed for the turn, off splits of :24, :48 1/5, and 1:11 2/5, Perret was already busy on Charon while the only movement Romero made was to check behind his right shoulder twice, going into the turn and coming out of it. He didn't look back again. He didn't have to.

Right before the wire, Romero, who had not even been extending his arms fully while riding her in the stretch, stood up. She crossed the finish line seven lengths ahead of Charon, getting the mile in 1:36 and completing the mile and a quarter in 2:00 4/5 on a track which was labeled "good." In doing so, she had broken Love Sign's 1980 Alabama Stakes record of 2:01 and missed General Assembly's 2:00 track record by four-fifths of a second, set when he won the 1979 Travers. Only one other Travers winner, Honest

Pleasure (2:00 1/5) in 1976, ever ran faster than Go for Wand did that day. She did it under wraps.

As she cruised to victory in effortless motion, Badgett simply watched in amazement. As Romero guided her to the winner's circle, the jockey held up his left index finger, indicating No. 1. "Incredible," he said. "I'll tell you one thing. She tied a stakes record. If I'd have just hit her one time, I would've broken it. It was no contest. She was in a league of her own."

That was now a consensus opinion. "I admire Bill Badgett and Mrs. du Pont Lunger for giving us the opportunity to run against them again," Charon's owner, Stanley Ersoff, said. "At this point, I think they had the filly championship sewed up, but they gave us another chance at their filly." Charon's trainer, Navarro, said, "It was a magnificent race. I don't mind losing. It will take a super horse to beat Go for Wand." Perret, who had gotten frequent views of Go for Wand's derriere, said, "That filly is a true champion, and she goes out and proves she is. My filly is a hell of a filly. In any other year she would be the best, but you can't take anything away from the winner."

And the winner would not challenge colts a week

later in the Travers. Mrs. Lunger laid that idea formally to rest. "I don't want her to do it," she said. "She'll meet the colts in the stud barn in two years."

She never made it.

## Taming Elders

After winning the Test, Go for Wand was ranked seventh in the weekly Thoroughbred Racing Communications (TRC) poll behind Criminal Type, Housebuster, Steinlen, Summer Squall, Prized and Unbridled. Bayakoa was eighth, followed by Safely Kept and Sunday Silence, who had just retired due to a ligament tear in his left foreleg. Two weeks earlier, Sunday Silence's rival, Easy Goer, had been retired because of a bone chip.

After her dominating run in the Alabama, Go for Wand climbed to third in the TRC poll, trailing only Criminal Type, who had received all forty first-place votes from participating media following his fourth consecutive grade I victory, and the brilliant sprinter Housebuster.

Suddenly, Go for Wand was one of the top contenders for Horse of the Year.

Badgett's long-term goal from day one of her three-year-old season was the Breeders' Cup Distaff. He had planned on running Go for Wand in the Alabama and then in one fall race at Belmont Park against older fillies and mares, either the Maskette on September 2 or the Beldame October 7. Both are grade I stakes. After her performance in the Alabama, Badgett had pretty much settled on the Beldame. Then Go for Wand changed his mind. She would go in the Maskette and the Beldame. "She was just doing so darn good, and the Maskette wasn't coming up an overwhelming race," Badgett said. "That was pretty much what made my final decision. Still, we waited until the last minute."

Bettors didn't seem to mind, sending Go for Wand off as the 3-10 favorite in a field of six which included another outstanding daughter of Deputy Minister, Open Mind, who was seeking to recapture the form which earned her an Eclipse Award as two-year-old filly champion in 1988 and three-year-old filly champion in 1989. Open Mind had raced just once since finishing third behind Bayakoa and Gorgeous in the 1989 Breeders' Cup Distaff, finishing fifth in the grade I Ballerina Stakes at Saratoga for trainer D. Wayne Lukas. But Go for

Wand would get a stronger challenge from Open Mind's stablemate in the Maskette, Feel the Beat, who had won two consecutive seven-furlong sprint stakes, including the grade I Ballerina Stakes. Proper Evidence, the winner of the previous year's Ballerina, Mistaurian, who had won the Vagrancy Handicap at Belmont, and Bold Wench completed the field.

The start of the Maskette mirrored the start of the Test, as Go for Wand broke slowly, then rushed up on the inside. Romero settled her into a comfortable second as Feel the Beat led through a demanding half-mile in :45 2/5. At one point, Feel the Beat increased her lead from one length to two, but Romero was sitting on a ton of horse and the rest of the field was far back.

Go for Wand cruised up to engage Feel the Beat in the far turn, took the lead at the top of the stretch, and, with a couple of taps from her rider, cruised home a two and a half-length winner, getting the mile in 1:35 3/5. Feel the Beat gamely held second by a nose over Mistaurian. Open Mind was last, nearly eleven lengths behind Go for Wand.

While Go for Wand's victory was not spectacular, it was certainly professional, kind of like an assassin's.

"She scares me," Romero said afterward. "She's so good. She's unbeatable now; she's a champion."

Badgett was a bit more subdued. "I'm glad to get by this one," he said.

The Beldame beckoned.

If the Alabama was a coronation, the Beldame was a revelation. Go for Wand, the 1-5 favorite, drew the outside post in a field of five. To her immediate inside was Colonial Waters. The other three had no impact on the race.

Colonial Waters and Go for Wand broke together and remained that way for three-quarters of a mile in the mile and an eighth stakes, Colonial Waters on the inside and Go for Wand glued to her flank. After a relatively easy :23 2/5 first quarter, they threw in a second quarter in :22 1/5, drawing away from the other three horses. They reached six furlongs in 1:09 1/5 and Go for Wand eased closer to Colonial Waters on th turn in a virtual replay of the Maskette. Only this tim she poured it on, even as Romero sat motionless her. She crossed the wire four and three-quart lengths ahead of Colonial Waters in a stakes rec 1:45 4/5, all of two-fifths of a second off Secreta 1973 track record. It may have been the fastest

and an eighth ever run by a filly in New York. "I never uncocked my stick that day," Romero said. "I knew she was really running, but she was doing it so easily. If I would have pushed her at all, she could have broken Secretariat's track record. But it would have been stupid to do that with another big race coming up. I didn't want to mess her up. I thought that was her best race ever."

Her victory pushed her career earnings to $1,373,338 in just twelve starts.

A photo of the Beldame by Eclipse Award-winning photographer Skip Dickstein which appeared in *The Blood-Horse* magazine caught her perfectly in mid-stride, all four legs off the ground as if she was flying; her beautiful blazed face looking straight ahead; her ears cocked back; her mane bristling in the breeze, and Romero just sitting there, his unused whip in his right hand.

Badgett struggled to find words afterwards. "I'm really proud of her," he said. "All of her races have been fantastic, but this was a great one."

The TRC weekly poll reflected that. Go for Wand, who had won five consecutive grade I stakes and six for the season, was now No. 1. Criminal Type, who had

been scheduled to race the day before the Beldame in the Jockey Club Gold Cup, had injured his left front ankle and was done for the year and ultimately retired. He garnered more first place votes in the poll than Go for Wand, seventeen to fifteen, but she accumulated more points, 318 to 286. Summer Squall was third at 254 and Bayakoa fourth at 231.

There would be only one race left in Go for Wand's season, the Breeders' Cup. The media had been asking Badgett for weeks if Go for Wand might forego the Distaff for the Classic in an attempt to clinch Horse of the Year. "Mrs. Lunger was totally against it, but I was thinking about it," Badgett recalled. "Maybe if it was somebody else's horse at the time, I would have definitely considered it. She was pretty adamant. She's from the old school, that fillies should run against fillies. She is very superstitious, too, so you're really bucking the system if you have to push things to get what you want. Rather than push, push, push all the time to run her against the boys, I kind of left it alone."

The press didn't. One columnist called Go for Wand's connections chicken-hearted for not going in a

Classic suddenly wide open with Criminal Type out of the race. The criticism might have stung Mrs. Lunger, but Badgett shrugged it off. "I think it bothered her a little more than me," Badgett said. "I kind of take that stuff with a grain of salt. You run your business; you do the best you can, and you try to do what's right for your horses. A lot of times you get talked out of things that you knew were the right things to do only because you're getting pressure from outside sources, the press or other sources. So you try not to let that happen."

He knew Go for Wand still would get tested.

Go for Wand was entered in the Distaff, where she would face the '89 Distaff winner, Bayakoa. "At the time, I honestly thought if she could have won that filly race, especially against Bayakoa, she could have been Horse of the Year, anyway," Badgett said. "She would have had quite a case on her side, too."

That case was rock solid, actually. If she won the Distaff against a proven champion, Go for Wand's 1990 record would have been eight wins, seven of them grade I stakes and the other a grade III, and one second in a grade I stakes in nine starts.

Who could have voted against that record?

The chilling reality is that if Badgett had raced her in the Classic against colts, and the same tragedy had ensued that cost Go for Wand her life, Badgett would have been run out of town.

## Death In The Afternoon

By 1990, the Breeders' Cup had become firmly established as the championship event of Thoroughbred racing. Since its first running in 1984, the then seven-race series had provided drama and spectacle on all levels. Breeders' Cup VII, on October 27 at Belmont Park, promised to deliver more of the same.

With Criminal Type out of the Classic, the Cup had one marquee match-up: Go for Wand against Bayakoa in the Distaff, a rare meeting of two champions who had never raced against each other. Bayakoa, a six-year-old Argentinean mare trained by Hall of Famer Ron McAnally, was named champion older female of 1989 after winning nine of eleven starts, one of them the Breeders' Cup Distaff. In 1990, she had won six of nine starts, two of the three losses against colts. For the second straight year, her owners, Frank and Jan

Whitham, supplemented Bayakoa to the Breeders' Cup at a cost of $200,000.

There was no better human interest story than the Badgetts, newlyweds who had delayed their honeymoon until after they sent out Go for Wand in the Breeders' Cup. A *Daily News* photo by Daniel Farrell, the man responsible for Rose meeting Badgett, appeared October 23, catching Go for Wand reaching down to nibble at the carrots in Rose's left hand. The next day, an Associated Press picture picked up by many newspapers showed Badgett and Rose standing and smiling with Go for Wand standing between them. That same day, *Newsday* ran a large picture of Go for Wand on her back — playfully rolling in dirt. Four days later, *Newsday*'s front page of its Sunday sports section would show her on her back again.

"It was just like a whirlwind, the attention that she got and that we got," Rose said. "They said this is the human interest story of the decade."

It was an even better story than the press knew. Though she told few people, Rose found out just before the Breeders' Cup that she was pregnant with the Badgett's first child. "We'd been together for several years," Rose said. "And we were excited about it. We already had bought a house and we were planning on children. But we weren't going to tell anybody until after the Breeders' Cup. I continued galloping her up to the Breeders' Cup. I wanted to get up to that race. When I got up on Go for Wand that morning, I knew win, lose or draw, that it would be the last time. She was going to South Carolina. She wouldn't race again until next year and I was going to have a baby. It seems so ironic. People saw what happened and must have thought our lives were over, when, in fact, they'd just begun. Things happen for a reason."

A crowd of 51,236 braved a brisk forty-three degrees to attend Breeders' Cup VII on a clear day at Belmont Park in Elmont, Long Island. Millions more watched on NBC-TV. An isolated camera was set up in Mrs. Lunger's box, where she and Rose would watch the Distaff together. Badgett would watch from the clubhouse because Mrs. Lunger's superstitions left him little choice. "From the day Go for Wand broke her maiden, we never watched the race together, me and Mrs. Lunger," Badgett explained in 1999. Being superstitious, Mrs. Lunger told the trainer he wasn't allowed to sit with her, so he ended

up watching the race from the apron. "Now I'm glad I did because I got out on the track very quickly."

The first Breeders' Cup race, the $1-million Sprint, had fourteen starters and twelve survivors. Mr. Nickerson, who was the 7-1 fourth choice under Chris Antley, suffered a heart attack and fell to the track near the far turn, never to get up. Shaker Knit, an 87-1 longshot under Jose Santos, had the misfortune of being in the wrong place at the wrong time — behind Mr. Nickerson when he went down. Shaker Knit fell over him and was put down that night.

The Breeders' Cup continued, and Santos won the next race, the $1-million Juvenile Fillies, by five lengths on the 1-5 favorite, Meadow Star, who completed a perfect seven-for-seven season.

The $1-million Distaff was next, without one of its top contenders: four-year-old Gorgeous, who chipped a bone in her left front knee while galloping the day before. She had run second in the 1989 Breeders' Cup Distaff behind Bayakoa; upset her in the Apple Blossom Handicap in April; and, in her last start, been second to Bayakoa in the Spinster Stakes at Keeneland. Seven fillies and mares remained, and the betting reflected how strongly Go for

Wand and Bayakoa were regarded. Go for Wand, going for her sixth consecutive stakes victory, went off the 3-5 favorite from the two post. Bayakoa, who would spot Go for Wand four pounds, was at even money under Laffit Pincay Jr. from the four post. Colonial Waters was next lowest in odds at 14-1. The other four were longshots: Mistaurian (35-1), Luthier's Launch (43-1), Valay Maid (55-1), and Flags Waving (74-1).

The two-horse battle was joined almost immediately. Go for Wand broke in mid-pack, but quickly rushed up on the inside to take the lead with Bayakoa settling in a tight second, right alongside her.

"I thought if she broke well, I'd take advantage of it," Romero said. "I really felt that Laffit thought I was going to follow him all the way around. But she broke good. I said, 'He's going to follow me.' I wasn't going to let him take me all over the racetrack and carry me out. I wanted to be in control."

And then the two champions went at it head to head, nose to nose. Romero bided his time, talking to his filly, then urging her on at the five-eighths pole. Pincay did the same. It became a cat and mouse game. At the five-sixteenths pole, Go for Wand had a half-length on her challenger. Pincay, meanwhile, was urging Bayakoa to give more.

"When he came up to me, I moved away from him again. Then he urged his horse again," Romero said. "I really had to set Go for Wand down, but I had some horse left."

Rose, watching from Mrs. Lunger's box, said, "Turning for home, I could see Randy had more horse. Then they both hit another gear. I knew she was going to be in it until the wire."

Although Go for Wand was still clinging to a narrow lead at the eighth pole, the two horses' strides were absolutely synchronized. They reached the sixteenth pole with Go for Wand still in front by maybe a head. "It was going to be a great finish," Romero said. "At the time, I was in control."

Then Go for Wand reached out for her next stride. For a reason nobody will ever know, Go for Wand's right ankle shattered when it hit the track.

She fell, catapulting Romero over her neck, and tumbled on the ground, her legs flailing as she rolled on her back.

Then she got up and struggled toward the finish line,

her broken right ankle swinging like a pendulum in a ghastly image imprinted for life on anyone who saw it. She reached the finish line and collapsed. Romero was still prone on the track.

"After I fell down, I looked out of the corner of my eye," Romero said. "I was on my side, eight fractured ribs and a hairline fractured shoulder. And I picked up my left arm, and I looked underneath my arm. I could see her leg flopping and I said, 'Oh, my God.' I put my head down. They picked me up in the stretcher."

Nine years later, he explained, "My mare was trying so hard, she stumbled. I really think she just stumbled. She ran as hard as she could and she fell down."

Badgett raced onto the track, but when he got to her, he knew she couldn't be saved. "I just get goose bumps thinking about it," he reflected. "I mean I was standing next to Swale eight days after the Belmont, sitting on the fence, the happiest person in the world. And the horse drops dead right in front of me. You accept stuff like that, but to her?"

She had always been sound. "Too sound," Badgett said in disbelief nine years later. "She didn't have anything wrong with her whatsoever.

"The worst part about the whole thing was you never see horses break down where she broke down, in deep stretch," he said. "If a horse is going to break down like that, they usually do it down the backside, where they're changing leads, or on the turn you see it a lot. But there? That's probably the worst part of the whole thing that I can talk about."

Even Ruffian's fatal accident in her 1975 match race against Foolish Pleasure had happened on the backstretch. Go for Wand was dying stark in front of the entire crowd.

As Go for Wand staggered the last remaining steps of her life, outrider Steve Erck did his thankless job. After reaching her, he wrapped his arms around Go for Wand's neck and steered her to the ground. "There's always a chance a horse might be saved," he told writer Jay Hovdey, then with the *Los Angeles Times*. "If that was the case, it was up to me to stop her before she ran into the rail or something else, and caused even more damage to herself. By the time I got her down, it looked to me like she'd broken both legs. But I couldn't really tell. All I saw was a lot of blood. And all the horse is thinking about is the pain — and getting it over with as soon as possible."

Millions on TV witnessed Rose's horror as Go for Wand went down. They saw Mrs. Lunger turn her back away from the tragedy she could watch no longer. Rose ran downstairs to her filly. "I wanted to get there and everybody was in my way," Rose said. "So many people. I made my way to the winner's circle. I went on the track. I wanted to hold her. People said, 'No, no, no.' She was looking at me. I was trying to talk to her and I was hysterical. Then, when I knew what they had to do, I said, 'Okay, okay.' And all of a sudden it was over. Then I didn't know what to do. I knew I had to get to her, but then what?

"Billy found me and said, 'Just keep walking, just keep walking.' Everybody was staring at us."

Richard Jones had run onto the track, too. "When I saw her fall down, I jumped over the rail and took off," he said. "I think I said to Bill, because Rose was hysterical, I said, 'Bill, you get Rose out of here.' Somebody had to give the order to put her down. I did. There was no shock then. You just deal with this one step at a time. Then we went back and cried our eyes out."

Jones had plenty of company. At the Badgett's Barn 41, her groom, Joe Schonstein, told reporters, "She's like my best friend. It's not like she's an animal; she's a person." Badgett's assistant, Tony Mitchell, said, "I know I'll never be around another filly like this in my lifetime."

The McAnallys, Ron and his wife, Debby, tried dealing with the flood of emotions following Bayakoa's six and three-quarter length victory over Colonial Waters. They took no satisfaction in the way it was won. "They give their lives for our enjoyment," Debby McAnally said. Her husband said merely, "I can't cope with this...That other filly..."

As Badgett guided Rose away from the track, he was at a loss for words. And then they were left to struggle to get through the night.

In the heat of the tragedy, questions were raised as people sought answers. Was the track unsafe? Did the two deaths in the Sprint have anything to do with her death? "Unfortunately, one horse has a heart attack," Badgett said in 1999. "Another horse pulled up bad. The track superintendent, Joe King, probably got a lot more criticism overall than he really deserved for a long period of time."

Badgett acknowledged that the track might have benefited from water as it had not rained for some weeks. The weather had been hot and humid, drying out the surface day after day. But Badgett placed no blame. "The track was safe and Go for Wand was in the best shape of her life," he said. "I'll always believe she was digging down too deep. It was the first time she had ever faced the kind of pressure Bayakoa applied. Bayakoa never gave my filly a breather. In the heat of the battle, Go for Wand planted her leg the wrong way...and it happened."

The Badgetts left the track and went home. Friends and family stopped by to offer their condolences through the interminable evening. The telephone rang incessantly. Rose was distraught, still reeling from the tension leading up to the race and the calamity that followed: "The cameras were on us so they could see our reaction. I was right there. At the house, I felt terrible. I couldn't even think of eating or sleeping. In my mind, I was so close to Go for Wand, maybe too close. Other people didn't know her like I did. I was very, very saddened. I kept thinking, 'How can Billy be so strong?' But I think that brought us closer together as husband and wife. A tragedy like this makes you realize how much you need each other."

Rose was still crying in bed when Badgett went to sleep. He whispered to her: "Think about the baby. Think about the nursery we're going to build. Think about the name we're going to pick. Think about the joy we're going to experience."

Time would allow them to remember all the joy they experienced with Go for Wand.

# EPILOGUE

## *Continuing*

A little more than two hours after he suffered eight broken ribs and a hairline fracture of his shoulder when Go for Wand went down, **Randy Romero** somehow found the strength to ride Izvestia in the $3-million Breeders' Cup Classic. "The adrenaline was flowing in my blood," he said. "I probably shouldn't have rode."

Izvestia, trained by Roger Attfield, went off the 5-1 third choice in the field of fourteen and finished sixth, ten lengths behind the winner, Unbridled.

Romero's career was never the same after that day. "My career never got back to its fullest," he said. "It never affected my riding, but I could never get back to the top."

Three and a half months after Go for Wand's accident, just days into his comeback, Romero broke his left elbow and left collarbone in an accident at Gulfstream Park. He suffered through a succession of surgeries over two and a half years, but doctors could not get the elbow to heal properly. He also rode briefly in Hong Kong in an attempt to re-charge his career. Romero announced his retirement in 1994, only to return to riding. His career spiraled downward and he was powerless to stop it. "The elbow injury crushed me," Romero said. "I lost all my clientele, and when I came back, I was never 100 percent. People couldn't keep riding me. Trainers couldn't use me any more."

And still he rode, until July 12, 1999, when he was honored, fittingly, at Evangeline Downs, which sponsored the $30,000 Cradle of Jockey Stakes. No less than seven other riders with strong ties to southern Louisiana attended, including one of the nation's leading riders, Shane Sellers.

"Today is all about Randy Romero," Sellers told Jeff Taylor in a story in *Daily Racing Form*. "It is not about Shane Sellers or any of the other riders who came in. Randy paved the way for us younger riders to leave Louisiana and do some good."

Joining Sellers were Ron Ardoin, E.J. Perrodin, Corey Lanerie, Ray Sibille, Mark Guidry and Marlon St. Julien, the jockey Romero now represents as an agent.

The jockeys were joined by Romero's family and friends to celebrate his contributions to racing. "Randy and I grew up riding the bushes together," Ardoin said. "We both got our starts professionally right here in Lafayette. I believe he was a year ahead of me when I had my bug. I felt really honored that he called me and asked me to be part of this."

It is a night Romero will never forget: "To go back to all the roots and all the people who started me out…It was a dream."

In a perfect world, Romero would have ridden three winners from his three mounts that night. Instead, none finished in the money.

He was sixth on his final mount, Awesome Explosion, in the $30,000 Cradle of Jockeys Stakes, won by Oscar Magic, ridden by Marlon St. Julien, now his first client. "I never won the Kentucky Derby," Randy said. "I always wanted to, but never could. I want to win the Derby through him."

Romero retired with 4,294 wins, 3,743 seconds and 3,313 thirds from 26,091 mounts and earnings of $75,264,066.

He won riding titles at Arlington Park, Belmont

Park, Delta Downs, Evangeline Downs, Fair Grounds, Gulfstream, Hialeah, Jefferson Downs, Keeneland, and Louisiana Downs.

More than the numbers, Romero won the respect of every horseman who witnessed his courage and drive. "There will never be another Randy," Sellers said.

Romero seems, finally, at peace with his retirement. "I've probably been on the ground more than any other jockey with injuries," he said. "In life, there's a time to stop. It was my time to stop. At first it was scary, but I'm glad I did."

Romero treasures his time riding Go for Wand. "Some great memories," he said. "The man who taught me to ride said, 'Don't fall in love with a horse,' but I couldn't help it. I fell in love with her. God almighty, what a great filly. She was big, strong, with a lot of heart. She had determination, the fight to get the job done. She was special."

So was the only jockey who ever rode her.

**Christiana Stables** continues to race in the 21st Century, and began 2000 with six two-year-olds and eleven yearlings, as well as twelve racehorses, eight with Jim Murphy and two apiece with both Jonathan

Sheppard and Frank Brothers. Badgett stopped training for Christiana when Mrs. Lunger decided some three years ago that she did not want to race in New York except for the six-week Saratoga meet. "I was sorry to leave him," Mrs. Lunger said. "But I didn't want to race in the spring in New York. I didn't want to come to Aqueduct and Belmont. I wanted to go to Keeneland and Maryland. He's a wonderful trainer, and I was sorry to leave him."

Actually, Mrs. Lunger asked Badgett if he wanted to train horses for her for just the Saratoga meet. Badgett declined. "That would mean taking them from another trainer," he said. "That wasn't fair to those people and it wouldn't be fair to me. So I said I'd be more than happy to do it for you, but I'd rather not. And she understood that."

**Billy Badgett** understood that the burden of handling Go for Wand's tragedy was placed on his shoulders immediately. And he did the only thing he could do: he continued. That's what horsemen do. They continue.

"I kind of put myself in a situation like I'm the captain of the ship going down," he said. "It devastated the barn; it devastated the help. So I took it upon myself to keep everybody upbeat, keep everyone focused and get them back on the program. It was very difficult, but that's just one of those things you have to do. It's almost like a member of your family dying. It's part of reality. You have to accept it and go on. Rose didn't handle it all that well. She took it to heart." Badgett would, too. "I don't think it really set in for me until everybody had gotten over it," he said. "Then I went off by myself. It was pretty devastating."

Badgett noted ruefully that he and Mrs. Lunger had planned to run Go for Wand as a four-year-old. "We were planning on running her one more year," Badgett said. "She would have been a phenomenal handicap filly the next year. She was extremely sound."

The day after the accident, Mrs. Lunger and Richard Jones worked out arrangements with the New York Racing Association to have Go for Wand buried in the infield near the winner's circle at Saratoga, where she had been so dominant. "It was Mrs. Lunger's decision," Badgett said. "I thought that was great. They have a beautiful monument there." Saratoga is also where Go for Wand was inducted into the Hall of Fame in 1996 and where the grade I Maskette Stakes was relocated and renamed in Go for Wand's honor. Go for Wand, of course, had been named 1990 champion three-year-old filly, while Criminal Type was Horse of the Year.

It didn't take long for the Badgetts and Mrs. Lunger to realize they were not grieving alone. "Oh, God, it was unbelievable," Badgett said. "Unbelievable. It just never stopped. Poems from twelve- and thirteen-year-olds. Letters, pictures. You kind of get in this little bit of a bubble where you don't really know the appreciation that's going on outside your barn or outside your racetrack. We knew she was a great filly. In the industry, everybody knew she was a great filly. But we couldn't believe the following she had from everybody outside the game. Rose still has a trunk full of letters, painted pictures, and poems. It was non-stop. It filled up a trunk."

Incredibly, just like his old boss Woody Stephens, Badgett had already planned the first vacation of his life, the Badgetts' honeymoon, before his star horse died. Woody and Lucille Stephens went to Alaska despite the death of Swale. Billy and Rose went to

Jamaica. "It helped," Rose said. "We were waiting for the plane in the terminal, a little bit in a daze, waiting with our tickets and our luggage in line. And this lady came up to us. She knew who we were. She said, 'Excuse me. We're going to move you up to first class. We know who you are.' It was really weird. We got off that long line with our suitcases and went up to first class. We were stunned. And then, that kept happening for a while. People recognized us. They called our names wherever we went. You go to the store. You go to the deli. People saying they were sorry. People were so nice."

Although her death seemed senseless and cruel, Go for Wand's tragedy had positive repercussions for future Breeders' Cup runners — and all racehorses.

The veterinary and racing communities moved quickly to set up an injury management plan, which was in place by the 1991 Breeders' Cup at Churchill Downs and remains in use today. It consists of an On Call program developed by the American Association of Equine Practitioners and a myriad of specialized equipment and trained staff to respond to injured horses.

The On Call program makes member veterinarians trained in media relations available to the press to explain injuries as well as to offer assistance to injured horses. State-of-the-art equipment, including equine ambulances and stabilizing braces, is on site at every Breeders' Cup.

Dr. George Mundy helped develop the injury management plan while serving as chief veterinarian for the Kentucky Racing Commission. As he explained it: "The plan is to a) have all the necessary equipment in place and have all the people involved in racetrack injury management well aware of what to do, and b) impart information in a timely manner to the broadcast and print media."

At every Breeders' Cup since 1991, high-tech Kimzey ambulances have been stationed at key spots along the racetrack. The Kimzey has hydraulic lifts that lower the floor to ground level, preventing further trauma to injured horses. A horse simply has to step forward, instead of up. In addition, the ambulance has a hydraulic partition that helps prop the horse so he does not need to use an injured limb for balance.

Veterinarians man the ambulances, and have at their ready high-tech leg splints and trauma boots to help stabilize injured horses while they are still on the track.

In 1991, two horses suffered injuries while running in Breeders' Cup races. Both horses were pulled up by their riders, and members of the injury management team responded immediately. Each horse had a Kimzey brace applied and each was vanned back to its respective stable in a Kimzey ambulance. The quick response was credited with mitigating further damage to the injured horses.

Go for Wand's gallantry continued to move people long after she died. On April 17, 1993, composer Jeffrey Schindler's "Thoroughbred Fanfare" was performed for the first time by the Prince George's Philharmonic of Maryland under conductor Amy Mills. Schindler's inspiration was a three-year-old filly who died on the racetrack. "I was deeply moved by the spirit Go for Wand showed when, even after snapping her foreleg in the stretch, she continued to strive for the finish line," Schindler said. "She was humanely destroyed on the track with her eyes still fixed on that goal. As a tribute to her memory, I have tried to create a triumphant and noble fanfare, an evocation to the almost other-worldly beauty of horses in motion, and the stretch drive and finish of a championship horse race."

The Badgetts have three children now, Brooke, Brandon, and Brian, ages nine, seven, and five. "They know about her," Rose said. "They know she was the horse who got hurt. Little by little, we've told them. When Bevo got hurt, they asked, 'Was it like Wanda?' We said, 'Yeah, but he's okay.' They haven't seen the tapes, but they know I was very upset about it. Obviously, it's still painful, but they know she's up in heaven, which is good. They all ride and they have their favorite horses at the barn."

Rose had a favorite. Billy, too. "She kind of knew that once she was around, her presence was felt," Badgett said. Even after she was around. Even after years.

If we can never separate her remarkable achievements and her gruesome accident, then let us remember both the way trainer Charlie Whittingham suggested her gravestone should read:

She died on the lead.

# Addendum

Following are a few of the letters and poems the Badgetts and Mrs. Lunger received from fans.

Dear Rose & Billy,

I'd like to offer my deepest condolences to you after what happened to Go For Wand. I was in Las Vegas for the Breeders' Cup watching the races with mostly a partisan Bayakoa crowd since Bayakoa is a West Coast horse. But everyone was really torn up, and there were a lot of watery eyes in the place. Myself and a lot of other people I talked to did not even cash the tickets we had on Bayakoa, as our own kind of way of paying tribute to your tremendous filly. It was pretty obvious to me and to everyone that Go For Wand was going to win. Every time Bayakoa came to her, she had some more left. I've been following racing for about 10 years now and your horse was the best and most game female horse I've ever seen, filly or mare. From her races last year with Stella Madrid to this year with Charon and last with Bayakoa, your filly always oozed with class and superiority.

I've cried a lot since the Breeders' Cup. Your horse

brought out something in me I didn't know was there, something a lot more important than cashing a winning ticket. So try to take heart even though she's gone now. Remember she'll live on in everyone's mind as one of the greatest horses anyone has ever seen in our lifetime or any other lifetime, for that matter.

Alec Bauer, Walnut, California

Dear Rose Badgett:

Late this afternoon my husband and I left lavender chrysanthemums at the finish line at Saratoga Racetrack for your filly. This is her first night home, and we wanted to leave a token of our admiration for her, a horse with such generosity of spirit, such depth of heart.

We saw Go For Wand race here in the summer, and we were on the rail near the finish line at Belmont on Saturday. Our hearts broke when she fell, and we still can't believe that horrible moment actually occurred. We know that as heartbroken as we feel, your pain — and that of those who lived with her — must be immeasurably worse. We want you to know that we mourn with you.

We mourn for Go For Wand. She deeply touched us

all. To have the moment when her greatness was revealed to be the moment of her fall is too much to bear. Maybe we'll make sense of this in days to come, but I don't see how. Our hearts will heal, but they will not be the same hearts. Perhaps, when we think of her, after this initial pain diminishes, we'll remember how she defined fineness and learn from her what heart is.

It is going to freeze tonight, and the chrysanthemums will undoubtedly die. It is going to warm up again tomorrow, though. We'll take some fresh flowers out to the track and, if we can slip in again, leave them at the finish line for your girl. Go For Wand is not alone here. Our thoughts will be with her, and with you all, for a long, long time.

Please be well.

With sincerest regards,
Jean A. Kristinat, Cambridge, N.Y.

Mr. and Mrs. Badgett & Mrs. Lunger,

On that day that was so chilly,
We said farewell to a special filly,
If were words could only reveal,

How we really feel …
So young, beautiful, courageous & fast
Your image slowly fades into the past
Always doing more than your part
You deliberately captured out unsuspecting hearts

What happened wasn't supposed to be,
Sadly we're left in sorrow to grieve
Now under His care and His grace,
Others will continue to race

Never able to fill your absence,
Your spirit will always make its presence
It's never easy to say goodbye,
Especially though emotional cries

We promise to remember & never second guess,
That you were simply one of the best
Rest comfortably now our precious one
For now … eternity and peace has come

Scott Gioia, Kari & Kevin Marinucci
Poughkeepsie, N.Y.

I cried today
It was a strange bond
Love for a thoroughbred
Go For Wand

From last year's Breeders'
Where she won the Cup
To this year's Beldame
It was nowhere — but up!

Secretariat's record was
In her grip
Even without the sting
Of Randy's whip
She came to this year's big challenge
Ready to roll
How could we know she'd
Pay such a toll
Only a champion,
With a heart of a saint
Could look Bayakoa in the eye
And not grow faint
Ready to dig in —

And give it her all
Then it happened —
A horrible fall!

Even her damaged leg
Couldn't keep her down
Pure heart made her stagger —
There wasn't a sound

Our world stood still,
"It's a terrible dream,"
Shaken to our senses
By the wails and screams

We loved you, dear Wand
The magic you spun
It gave us great joy
To see you run
Maybe someday there
Will be another
Who touches us like
A sister or a brother

Till that day comes
With memories fond
We'll cherish the moments
Of the beautiful Wand

So Billy, Rose, Randy
Mrs. Lunger and team
Thanks for sharing with us
Your most treasured dream.

Joe Baal

# GO FOR WAND's PEDIGREE

| | | | |
|---|---|---|---|
| DEPUTY MINISTER, dkb/br, 1979 | Vice Regent, 1967 | Northern Dancer, 1961 | Nearctic<br>Natalma |
| | | Victoria Regina, 1958 | Menetrier<br>Victoriana |
| | Mint Copy, 1970 | Bunty's Flight, 1953 | Bunty Lawless<br>Broomflight |
| | | Shakney, 1964 | Jabneh<br>Grass Shack |
| GO FOR WAND, bay filly, April 6, 1987 | | | |
| OBEAH, b, 1965 | Cyane, 1959 | Turn-to, 1951 | Royal Charger<br>Source Sucree |
| | | Your Game, 1948 | Beau Pere<br>Winkle II |
| | Book of Verse, 1956 | One Count, 1949 | Count Fleet<br>Ace Card |
| | | Persian Maid, 1947 | Tehran<br>Aroma |

# GO FOR WAND'S RACE RECORD

**Go for Wand** — **b. f. 1987, by Deputy Minister (Vice Regent)–Obeah, by Cyane** — **Lifetime record: 13 10 2 0 $1,373,338**

**Own.– Christiana Stable**
**Br.– Christiana Stables (Pa)**
**Tr.– William Badgett Jr**

| Date/Race | Track | Fractions | Age | Race | PP | St | 1st | 2nd | Str | Fin | Jockey | Wt | Odds | Speed-Var | Top finishers | Comment | Field |
|---|---|---|---|---|---|---|---|---|---|---|---|---|---|---|---|---|---|
| 27Oct90- 5Bel | fst 1⅛ | :46$^2$ 1:10$^3$ 1:35$^4$ 1:49$^1$ | 3↑ | ⒻBC Distaff-G1 | 2 | 1 | 1½ | 1$^{hd}$ | 1½ | - | Romero RP | 119 | *.70 | -- | Bayakoa1236¾Colonial Waters1232½Valay Maid119$^{nk}$ | Fell | 7 |
| 7Oct90- 8Bel | fst 1⅛ | :45$^3$ 1:09$^1$ 1:33$^1$ 1:45$^4$ | 3↑ | ⒻBeldame-G1 | 5 | 2 | 2½ | 2½ | 12 | 14¾ | Romero RP | 119 | *.10 | 105-09 | GoforWnd1194¾ColonialWtrs1238¾BuythFrm1232¼ | Ridden out | 5 |
| 2Sep90- 8Bel | fst 1 | :23 :45$^2$ 1:09$^4$ 1:35$^3$ | 3↑ | ⒻMaskette H-G1 | 1 | 2 | 21½ | 2½ | 11 | 12½ | Romero RP | 118 | *.30 | 91-13 | GoforWnd1182½FeeltheBeat123$^{no}$Misturn1164 | Good handling | 6 |
| 11Aug90- 8Sar | gd 1¼ | :48$^1$ 1:11$^2$ 1:36 2:00$^4$ | | ⒻAlabama-G1 | 3 | 1 | 11 | 12 | 12½ | 17 | Romero RP | 121 | *.50 | 100-09 | Go for Wand1217Charon12148Pampered Star121 | Ridden out | 3 |
| 2Aug90- 8Sar | fst 7f | :22$^1$ :44$^3$ 1:08$^1$ 1:21 | | ⒻTest-G1 | 2 | 8 | 2½ | 2$^{hd}$ | 11½ | 12 | Romero RP | 124 | *1.20 | 100-05 | GoforWnd1242ScreenProspect1182¼TokenDnce1182½ | Driving | 10 |
| 10Jun90- 8Bel | fst 1⅛ | :46 1:10$^2$ 1:35$^3$ 1:48$^4$ | | ⒻMother Goose-G1 | 6 | 2 | 21 | 21½ | 11½ | 11¼ | Romero RP | 121 | *.80 | 90-20 | GoforWand1211¼Charon1214¼StellaMadrid1212¾ | Wide,driving | 6 |
| 4May90- 9CD | my 1⅛ | :48$^1$ 1:13 1:39 1:52$^4$ | | ⒻKy Oaks-G1 | 1 | 4 | 42 | 31½ | 22 | 23 | Romero RP | 121 | *.30 | 81-20 | Seaside Attraction1213Go for Wand1213Bright Candles1212½ | Flattened out | 10 |
| 21Apr90- 8Kee | my 1$\frac{1}{16}$ | :24$^3$ :48$^2$ 1:12$^2$ 1:43$^3$ | | ⒻAshland-G1 | 5 | 3 | 1½ | 11½ | 14 | 15 | Romero RP | 121 | *.30 | 88-12 | Go for Wand1215Charon1217½Piper Piper1128 | Driving | 5 |
| 10Apr90- 8Kee | my *7f | 1:26$^2$ | | ⒻBeaumont-G3 | 6 | 2 | 32 | 3$^{nk}$ | 14½ | 18½ | Romero RP | 122 | *.40 | 95-05 | GoforWand1228½Trumpet's Blare119$^{hd}$SeasideAttraction119½ | Ridden out | 6 |
| 4Nov89- 5GP | fst 1$\frac{1}{16}$ | :23$^4$ :47$^2$ 1:12 1:44$^1$ | | ⒻBC Juv Fillies-G1 | 4 | 5 | 63½ | 43½ | 31 | 12¾ | Romero RP | 119 | 2.50 | 90-01 | GoforWnd1192¾SweetRoberta119½StellaMdrd1192 | Drew clear | 12 |
| 14Oct89- 7Bel | fst 1 | :23 :45$^4$ 1:11 1:38$^4$ | | ⒻFrizette-G1 | 6 | 2 | 21 | 22 | 22½ | 2½ | Romero RP | 119 | *1.00 | 70-26 | StellaMdrd119½GoforWnd1195¼DncColony1191¾ | Finished well | 7 |
| 2Oct89- 2Bel | sly 1 | :23$^1$ :46$^2$ 1:11$^4$ 1:36$^3$ | | ⒻAlw 32000 | 9 | 1 | 11½ | 13 | 16 | 118¼ | Romero RP | 116 | *1.50 | 82-26 | GoforWand11618¼InFullCry116½Jen'sWish1166 | Ridden out | 9 |
| 14Sep89- 2Bel | fst 6f | :22$^1$ :45$^2$ 1:10$^3$ | | ⒻMd Sp Wt | 6 | 3 | 33 | 11 | 12½ | 14 | Romero RP | 117 | 2.40 | 86-15 | Go for Wand1174Nina1171½Worth Avenue117$^{nk}$ | Drew clear | 9 |

# Index

# Photo Credits

*Cover photo*: (Dan Johnson)

*Page 1:* Go for Wand winning the Mother Goose (Bob Coglianese); portrait (Barbara D. Livingston)

*Page 2:* Obeah (The Blood-Horse); Deputy Minister (Tony Leonard); Cyane (Allen W. Hopkins); Vice Regent (The Blood-Horse)

*Page 3:* Jane Lunger (Matt Goins/Equipix); Christiana Stable (The Blood-Horse); Mrs. Lunger with Billy Badgett and Randy Romero (Anne M. Eberhardt)

*Page 4:* Billy Badgett (Matt Goins/Equipix); Billy and Rose Badgett with Go for Wand (AP/Wide World Photos)

*Page 5:* Rose Badgett and Go for Wand (Shigeki Kikkawa)

*Page 6:* Randy Romero (Skip Dickstein); in winner's circle (The Blood-Horse); signing autographs (Evangeline Downs)

*Page 7:* Stella Madrid's Frizette (Barbara D. Livingston); Go for Wand's Breeders' Cup Juvenile Fillies (Skip Dickstein)

*Page 8:* Nearing the wire in the Breeders' Cup (Dan Johnson); wearing the floral blanket (Barbara D. Livingston)

*Page 9:* Winning the Beaumont (Bill Straus/Keeneland); winning the Ashland (The Blood-Horse); post parade (Anne M. Eberhardt)

*Page 10:* Seaside Attraction's Kentucky Oaks (Milton Toby); in the Belmont paddock (Barbara D. Livingston); winning the Mother Goose (Skip Dickstein)

*Page 11:* Getting a bath (Barbara D. Livingston); winning the Test (Skip Dickstein)

*Page 12:* Winning the Alabama (Barbara D. Livingston); No. 1 (Skip Dickstein)

*Page 13:* Winning the Maskette (Bob Coglianese); Looking back (Skip Dickstein)

*Page 14:* Winning the Beldame (Skip Dickstein); at the barn (Barbara D. Livingston)

*Page 15:* Breeders' Cup Distaff (Anne M. Eberhardt)

*Page 16:* Go for Wand's grave (Skip Dickstein); Rose Badgett up (Barbara D. Livingston)

# *Acknowledgments and Dedication*

Rose and Billy Badgett were wonderful sharing their time and their story, which meant revisiting some painful memories. They did so with unerring class and dignity. For those reasons, I dedicate this book to Billy, Rose, and Wanda.

Mrs. Lunger and Richard Jones also did interviews. Tom Gilcoyne and Dick Hamilton of the National Museum of Racing Hall of Fame came up with extremely helpful resource material as did Joan Lawrence and Jennifer Van Deinse of the National Thoroughbred Racing Association Media Office, and Judy Marchman and my editor, Jackie Duke, at Eclipse Press. The media relations office of the New York Racing Association was also helpful.

My wife, Anna, and our son, Bubba (a.k.a. Benjamin), listened through many versions of the manuscript and were supportive and helpful as were my proofreaders, Yale Sussman and Bob Gersowitz.

# ABOUT THE AUTHOR

Bill Heller, a freelance writer in Albany, New York, won the 1997 Eclipse Award for Magazine Writing for his story, "The Times They Are a-Changin' ", in *The Backstretch* magazine. He also is a three-time winner of the John Henry Award for Harness Racing Magazine Writing. He currently writes for the *Thoroughbred Times* and *The Backstretch*. Heller has authored nine other books, including *Obession: Bill Musselman's Relentless Quest*; *Overlay, Overlay*; *The Will To Win: The Ron Turcotte Story*; *Travelin' Sam, America's Sports Ambassador*; *Billy Haughton: The Master*; and *Playing Tall: The 10 Shortest Players in NBA History*.

Forthcoming titles
in the
THOROUGHBRED
Legends®

series:

**Seattle Slew**

**Native Dancer**

**Forego**

**Nashua**

**Spectacular Bid**

**John Henry**

Available titles

**Man o' War**

**Dr. Fager**

**Citation**

*Editor* — Jacqueline Duke
*Assistant editor* — Judy L. Marchman
*Book design* — Brian Turner